lifelight

lifelight

lifelight

lifelight

Light and Colour for Health and Healing

lifelight

Dr Penny Stanway

lifelight

KYLE CATHIE LIMITED

I dedicate this book to my father, John Avenel Rench, who was a true Renaissance man. For it was his delight in viewing the moon and stars, his thrill over each little glow-worm in the garden, and his fascination with physics, that lit my lifelong love of light and colour.

Acknowledgements

With warm thanks to the many people who have shared their knowledge and enthusiasm about light and colour with me. Thanks to Mark Buckingham, the designer, for his artistic flair; Caroline Taggart, my editor, for her encouragement and expertise; and Georgina Burns for her doggedness in finding just the right photographs.

First published in Great Britain in 2001 by
Kyle Cathie Limited
122 Arlington Road
London NW1 7HP
general.enquiries@kyle-cathie.com
www.kylecathie.com

ISBN 1 85626 409 2

Edited by Caroline Taggart
Design and illustrations by Mark Buckingham
Production by Lorraine Baird and Sha Huxtable
See also photographic acknowledgements on page 160

Dr Penny Stanway is hereby identified as the author of this work in accordance with Section 77 of the Copyright, Designs and Patents Act 1988.

A Cataloguing in Publication record for this title is available from the British Library.

Printed in Singapore by Kyodo Printing Co Pte Ltd

CONTENTS

INTRODUCTION

Light can thrill and delight. Just think of dancing sunbeams, a rainbow, or the romance of candlelight, starlight or moonlight. And light can be awesome. Indeed, many people describe God in terms of light, and speak of the 'dark night of the soul' when spiritual enlightenment seems far away. More down-to-earth but also vitally important, light is essential for our everyday health and well-being. This book describes what light does for us. It also shows how we can best enjoy its many benefits while at the same time keeping its negative effects in check. And it looks at our need for darkness.

Many people today are confused about whether sunlight is a friend or a foe, but here you'll find clear information about its pros and cons for your health. You'll also see practical ways of discovering the balance and intensity of daylight, electric light and colour that are right for you.

My research has crossed many professional boundaries, looking at the work of ophthalmologists, ophthalmic surgeons, cancer surgeons, dermatologists, scientists, opticians, optometrists, psychologists, philosophers, priests, colour therapists, interior designers, beauty therapists, and even crystal therapists and feng shui consultants. This is because light and colour affect so many aspects of everyday life, health and wellbeing, as well as so many disorders and illnesses. But while so many professionals are involved – and although we can learn a lot from each of them – they don't yet speak the same language. And this is partly what makes learning about light so challenging and fascinating.

Light is a vital part of our life. It consists of waves of electromagnetic radiation that enable us to see 10 million or so different colours. Some light comes from man-made electricity, lasers and explosions, and from natural sources such as lightning, fire and far-flung stars. But most comes directly from our nearest star – the sun. Light's energy gives us warmth and food. Sunlight's infrared rays heat the Earth and its atmosphere each day, and its visible and ultraviolet rays enable plants to grow, providing vegetables, fruit, nuts, seeds and grains for us to eat, fodder for our animals, and oil and other fuels to warm us through cold nights and winters. Without light we would freeze and starve.

Thanks to visible light we can see the world around us. This is true for most other animals too, though some creatures can also see certain other electromagnetic waves, such as infrared and ultraviolet, which we can't. We can see because little parcels of light energy enter our eyes and bleach pigments in light-sensitive nerve cells in the retina at the back of the eye, which then sends messages to the brain. Our eyesight doesn't work, as the

Greek philosopher Pythagoras thought in the fifth century BC, by rays coming out of our eyes! The experience of seeing has a huge extra benefit. It lets us create an inner world of pictures through our imagination, dreams and visually stored memories. But none of this is the whole story. Messages about light also enable the brain to balance the levels of almost every hormone and neurotransmitter (nerve-signal messenger), so influencing such vitally important things as our mood, energy, sexuality, weight, temperature, blood pressure, fertility and body clock.

As for light on the body, we constantly hear the dangers of too much sun – which is quite right – but we're not so often told of its many benefits. For example, UV creates vitamin D in the skin. It also influences our immunity to infection and several important cancers. Scientists suspect that while too much UV can increase the risk of skin cancers, moderate amounts may help protect us from skin cancer and some other cancers too, such as oestrogen-sensitive breast cancer and testosterone-sensitive prostate cancer. But that's not all. Light on the skin can even influence our body clock, helping our body rhythms stay in sync with those of people around us.

Light's many benefits are becoming ever clearer, but at the same time we are realizing that some of us aren't getting enough light ... and some of us are getting too much. We are also much more aware that different sorts of light may be particularly useful when treating certain conditions or ailments. Part Two of this book looks briefly at some of the many ways of using light or some of its wavelengths as treatments. Medical and surgical light therapies are used in increasing numbers of centres nowadays for a wide variety of common and not-so-common ailments. But we'll also look at some of the various complementary and alternative therapies involving light and colour, and see how these marry up with what orthodox health professionals can do, and with everyday common sense.

In Part Three, you'll find some of the many ailments that respond to light in one way or another. Each entry has specific suggestions on how to use light and colour to help you feel better. But because these are obviously not the only useful treatments, you'll also find other tips, along with suggestions that are specifically medical. And finally, there's a helplist of some of the many useful organizations involved with light.

The American optometrist Jacob Liberman came to fame by calling light 'the medicine of the future'. Now we can go further, because light is the medicine of today.

part one Light in your life

Everything we see is thanks to our eyes' amazing ability to receive light and relay information to the brain. The way the eye receives light is akin to how a camera works. Just as we can alter the amount of light entering a camera by changing its aperture so as not to over- or under-expose photographs, so too can each eye alter the amount of light passing through the pupil so we get the optimal amount of light on the retina. We can focus a camera to get clear photographs, and the eye can focus light on the retina. And just as light leaves its imprint on the emulsion coating of a film, so also does it leave its 'message' on the retina. However, unlike film, which we use only once, we use our retinas again and again to create images that change in fractions of a second, all day, every day, all life long. This is the miracle that makes the eyes vastly better than the most impressive camera.

Apart from enabling vision, light has major influences on hormones and neurotransmitters (substances that enable nerves to carry messages). This helps keep our mind and body working in a balanced way. And though it isn't fashionable to speak of a suntan as an asset, and too much sun is bad for us, nonetheless many millions of us enjoy being in the sun and reap good health if we do it safely.

Light – whether it comes directly from the sun or from electric light, gaslight, firelight, or the 'bioluminescence' from many living organisms – is a form of energy, and as such can have profound effects. The intensity of light entering our eyes and landing on our skin, and the timing of our exposure to light and darkness, are both important to our wellbeing, as are the various proportions of wavelengths present in 'white' light.

As for colours, not only can they give us pleasure but also, as modern science is discovering, and colour therapists have recognized for a long time, they can have important physical, emotional and spiritual effects.

In Part One, we'll look at how we receive, perceive and use light, as well as where light comes from, what it is, and how it gives us energy. We'll consider different lighting, and how light affects our health, mood, energy, sexuality, fertility and weight. We'll examine why light is often used as a metaphor for God, or for spiritual understanding or enlightenment. And we'll see how certain things can influence our light sensitivity.

Chapter 1
Light up your life

Light is vital for our physical, mental, emotional and spiritual health, and for our understanding and enjoyment of life. We receive light through our eyes and our skin. Our eyes gather data about the shape and colour of the world around us and relay it to the brain. They also receive information about the intensity of light and the timing of day and night, and pass this on to the brain. And the skin absorbs light and allows certain wavelengths to penetrate its surface.

The brain's visual cortex reacts to the eyes' messages, enabling us to see our surroundings. Messages also travel to other parts of the brain where they stimulate important changes in hormones and neurotransmitters. However, images originating in the outside world aren't the only ones we see. Our mind's eye allows us to 'see' images which come courtesy of our imagination, memory, and phenomena such as hallucinations and dreams. These self-generated images, or inner vision, are often full of vivid light and colour.

Not only do we see light around us and create images in our mind's eye, but also our cells – in common with those of many other living organisms – can actually produce tiny emissions of light. Certain individuals even claim to see an aura of light around each person.

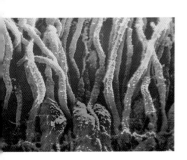

This may look like a coral reef, but it is actually an electron micrograph of the human retina, showing three colour-sensitive cones (falsely coloured orange) and a larger number of brightness-sensitive rods (falsely coloured green).

How we receive light

We receive light through our eyes and through our skin.

Light in the eyes

When light enters the eye it passes through the transparent cornea, the clear fluid in the front of the eye, and the hole in the iris called the pupil. It then travels on through the lens, which contains transparent proteins called crystallins, and makes the rays slant inwards. The ciliary muscles control the degree of slant by changing the shape of the lens.

Next, rays go through the clear gel in the back of the eye and come to a focus on the retina – a layer of nerve cells 32mm (1¼in) across and 250 microns deep – which coats the inside of the back of the eye.

The retina's nerve cells are sensitive to light. Stimulation of these 'photoreceptors' by light generates a small electrical charge that travels as an electro-chemical message along some of the million or so fibres in the optic nerve to the brain's visual cortex, in the back of the skull.

There are two types of photoreceptors:
● 125 million 'rods' scattered around the retina let us see in black, white and grey in dim light. They also let us see things on the periphery of our vision. They contain red pigments (rhodopsins, or 'visual purple', made from vitamin A – for food sources, see pages 108–109) which are broken down in light by being bleached. Used pigments are mostly replaced at night.

● Seven million 'cones', mostly in the centre of the retina, particularly in a yellow spot called the macula, provide detail and – when light is bright enough – colour. There are three types, each containing one of three pigments, one letting us perceive certain wavelengths as red, one as green, and one as blue; when red- and green-sensitive cones are equally stimulated, we see yellow. Each group of light wavelengths entering the eye produces a particular combination of signals from the three types of cone, allowing us to perceive millions of different colours.

While 80 per cent of the retina's light messages stimulates the visual cortex, providing eyesight, about 20 per cent stimulates the brain's hypothalamus. And this, as we'll see, affects both our physical and our emotional wellbeing.

Whether light affects the hypothalamus or not in people who are blind or partially blind, depends on how their condition affects their eyes. In someone with age-related macular degeneration, for example, light continues to provide some stimulation to the hypothalamus because this condition doesn't affect the rods. However, a cataract reduces the amount of light – especially blue light – reaching the retina, which in turn reduces the stimulation of the hypothalamus. With another condition, retinitis pigmentosa, stimulation may also be reduced, depending on how many rods are affected. Damage to the optic nerve by, for example, multiple sclerosis, can also reduce the stimulation of the hypothalamus.

Light on the skin

Much light bounces off the skin. But a little enters and this, as we'll see later, has some vitally important effects.

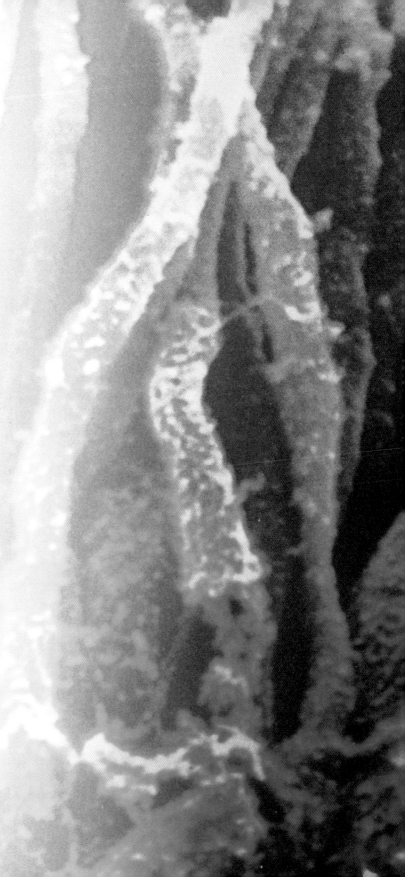

How we perceive light

We perceive images using 'outer vision' or 'inner vision', though sometimes the distinction isn't entirely clear.

'Outer vision'

Light messages from outside activate the visual cortex, the part of the brain which assembles images of what we see. Other parts of the brain interpret their meaning, unless we 'see without seeing' – for example, when someone drives miles without knowingly seeing anything. If we look at something bright, then turn away, we see its 'after image'.

People with short, long or far sight, or astigmatism, perceive blurred images, while a cataract clouds vision, and glaucoma (high eye-fluid pressure) gives things a pale grey cast. Some people have 'tunnel vision', seeing only straight ahead; others have only peripheral vision. Some totally blind people may, one day, benefit from a 'bionic eye' which creates images directly in the brain.

The hypothalamus receives light messages via the eyes, and a little light energy via the skull. And although it is so tiny it does some extremely important jobs.

'Inner vision'

Some people have a photographic memory, while others think in non-visual concepts. Also, our imagination can distort memorized images. And we can use our memory and imagination to create images in our waking moments and our dreams.

Most totally blind people once had some vision which 'primed' their brain to see images, making visual imagination possible. However, those totally blind since birth had no priming and so can't imagine pictorial images of the outside world. However, they may see patterned light produced by the spontaneous firing of visual-cortex cells.

Seeing stars

Pressure on the eyeball, a sudden head movement or a blow to the head can all stretch the retina, producing flashes or 'stars'. We also see less dramatic sensations of light – phosphenes – when we close our eyes.

Visual hallucinations and psychedelia

Hallucinations seem to come from the outside world but have no external stimulus, and aren't provoked by the imagination either.

Psychedelia is a rapid kaleidoscopic succession of vividly coloured images, often patterned or coloured, seen in the mind's eye. One trigger is spontaneous visual-cortex activity immediately before sleep. Another is irritation by a fever, alcohol, lack of oxygen, changes in blood-vessel diameter before a migraine (producing a migraine aura), 'Lewy-body' dementia (see page 140), or hallucinogenic substances such as LSD (lysergic acid diethylamide), 'magic' mushrooms and the vapour from certain glues.

Ghosts

No one knows whether seeing ghosts involves perceiving light from a paranormal phenomenon or seeing an image created by the unconscious mind.

Near-death experiences

Some people who've been on the brink of death describe travelling down a dark tunnel towards a bright light. Some see a welcoming relative and sense feelings of peace and no return. Whether this is a premature view of the afterlife or a phenomenon created by oxygen-starved brain cells is unknown.

Synesthesia

In some people, mostly women, one sensation stimulates another. Music, for example, may make them 'see' colours, deep notes eliciting red and high-pitched ones blue. This 'colour-hearing' may be a learned phenomenon but it's fascinating that ancient Chinese wisdom considers both deep notes and red to influence the base chakra (see pages 19 and 43), and both high notes and blue to influence the 'third eye' chakra.

Slightly deaf people hear better in the light than in the dark, and sound can make vision sharper.

How we use light

Messages about light received by the visual cortex allow us to see. Those received by the hypothalamus, the pituitary and pineal glands, and the limbic system influence nearly every body system. And light on the skin can produce pigment to protect the skin, create vitamin D, influence immunity and several hormones, and even affect the body clock.

Hypothalamus and pituitary gland

The cherry-sized hypothalamus is linked with the pituitary, and both these 'master' glands help regulate our hormones and neurotransmitters. The hypothalamus uses data about light, other external sensations, and internal body functions to:

1. Balance the actions of the autonomic nervous system, which runs basic body functions without our conscious control. This affects heart rate, digestion, blood pressure, temperature control, appetite and thirst, fluid balance, stress level, emotions and immunity.

2. Balance its production of hormones that trigger the release of pituitary hormones. These include melanocyte-stimulating hormone, prolactin, 'feel-good'

endorphins, and hormones which stimulate the thyroid and adrenal glands, and the ovaries or testes.

3. Influence the pineal gland.

Pineal gland

This tiny cone-shaped structure in the centre of the skull is sometimes called the 'third eye', and is very sensitive to light.

● Messages about light act on an amino acid called tryptophan (for food sources, see page 82) to make a neurotransmitter called serotonin (5-hydroxytryptamine, or 5-HT). Serotonin is probably more widely active than any other neurotransmitter in the brain. It's involved in the sleep-wake cycle, temperature regulation, sensory perception, sexual behaviour, reproduction and movement. It also affects mood, appetite and blood pressure, and helps regulate the level of cortisol, an adrenal hormone.

● When it's dark, the lack of messages about light acts on serotonin to make a hormone called melatonin (see pages 72–3) and pump it into the blood. Melatonin suppresses pituitary-hormone production but boosts the levels of 'feel-good' endorphins.

Limbic system

This is a network of nerve-cell clusters in the brain which uses messages about light to help regulate the body's production of adrenaline and noradrenaline, and to influence our emotions.

Skin

When light's ultraviolet rays enter the skin, they boost the production of its pigment, melanin, leading to a suntan. Light also heats the skin, makes its oils more antiseptic, and encourages wound healing. But light doesn't just have local effects, it also lowers the body's cholesterol level and helps produce two hormones – 'vitamin' D (which acts just like a hormone, though it isn't produced by an endocrine gland) and testosterone. Messages induced by light on the skin even reach the brain's body clock. And some completely blind people can recognize that there is light on their skin even when it lacks infrared heat.

Red light penetrates more deeply than blue, and brighter light penetrates more deeply than dimmer light. A tiny amount travels right through the body – as you can see if you put your hands over your eyes in very bright light, when you'll see red light coming through. A minute amount of light can even go through the skull. And the blood distributes some of the energy from light on the skin to every part of the body.

Sunlight on the skin doesn't just make us warm and tanned – it also wards off certain skin infections, helps wounds heal, lowers cholesterol, helps produce vitamin D and testosterone, and influences the body clock.

How we create light

The light on this planet doesn't only come from the sun, fire or electric light. Some plants and animals – including 90 per cent of deep-sea creatures – create light by bioluminescence.

Bioluminescence

This light results from the oxidation of substances called luciferins that are probably ingested in food. In land animals bioluminescent light is usually green, yellow or red. In marine organisms it's usually blue-green or green, and in some it even flashes in particular sequences. Bioluminescence can illuminate or attract prey or mates, camouflage or act as a decoy, or frighten predators or make them vulnerable. Bioluminescent organisms include:

● Some plankton, which create marine phosphorescence called 'sailors' fire'.

● Some squid or shrimp, which produce glowing clouds of phosphorescent substances.

● Lanternfish, which have luminescent organs along their body.

● Anglerfish, which have luminescent bacteria in an organ dangling from their forehead.

● Flashlight fish, which have luminescent bacteria in their cheeks.

● Black loosejaw fish, which produce red and blue light.

● Honey fungus, which gives a green light to rotting wood.

● Jack o'lantern toadstools, which glow.

● Glow-worm beetles, which produce light as bright as a hi-fi's LED display.

● Fireflies, which create light brighter than that of a glow-worm.

● Some jellyfish, clams, sharks, worms, snails and centipedes.

Humans don't bioluminesce as such but our cells, like those of all living organisms, create tiny amounts of light in the form of 'parcels' of energy called photons. They are recordable by sophisticated measuring devices, and in total darkness even single photons are visible by humans as tiny particles of light.

The body's energy also reveals itself in movements, heat, smells, sounds, thoughts, and changes in the colour and brightness of skin, hair and eyes. Most of us can easily

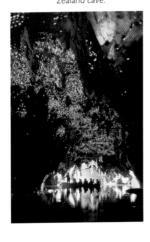

The people in this boat are admiring an extraordinarily beautiful display of light produced by firefly beetles trying to attract mates in a New Zealand cave.

recognize when someone's energy level is high or low.

All this energy creates an electromagnetic field (emf) around the body that can be measured with an emf meter up to 4m (13ft) away. It can also be viewed with Kirlian photography (which records interference between the body's emf and an electrically charged plate), or a PIP scan (done with polycontrast interference photography that records interference between our emf and full-spectrum light around us).

Auras

A few individuals can see a pulsating aura of light and colour around the body, which probably represents the body's emf. They say its thickness, symmetry and colour are a blueprint of the owner's health and wellbeing, and rapidly change with illness or imbalance.

They describe six layers ('bodies'), including the etheric (said to be influenced by and to influence physical health), which is 2cm (³⁄₄in) outside the body; the astral (said to concern thoughts and emotions), 30cm (1ft) further out; and the spiritual (said to represent spiritual development), 1m (about 3ft 3in) or more further still.

Traditional Chinese wisdom teaches that the aura has seven main chakras – energy centres which vibrate at particular frequencies (hence their association with particular colours), allow energy to pass between the aura's layers, and reflect and influence the health of hormone glands and nearby structures. There is some scientific evidence that these do indeed exist. Some colour therapists aim to adjust 'unbalanced' chakras with coloured light.

Chapter 2
Light unwrapped

Almost all our 'skylight' – the light that illuminates us from the sky – comes from the sun; only a little is from other stars. But sunlight is just a small part of the sun's electromagnetic energy; we also receive solar energy in the form of infrared, ultra-violet and other invisible radiation, including cosmic rays.

The sun's light and heat enable plants, humans and other animals to grow and thrive. And we can burn coal, oil and peat (partially decomposed vegetable matter) to give us energy for such things as heating, cooking, electric lighting and transport. Without sunlight, all living things on Earth would soon die.

While sunlight gives us life, its various sub-fractions – the wavelengths we perceive as colours – have important influences on our health. When they reach the body they aren't just reflected away but enter the body through the eyes and the skin. One reason we feel different, physically and emotionally, according to the season of the year, the amount of cloud and pollution, and the time of the day, is because each of these variables affects the proportions of sunlight's various wavelengths or 'colours'.

Sunlight

Virtually all our natural light comes from sunlight's energy waves. These have no mass but do exert very slight pressure: just outside the atmosphere this is 1 kilogram per square kilometre (2.2lb per 0.6 sq mile) – enough to propel a space sailship!

The e-m spectrum

The sun's electromagnetic (e-m) energy waves differ according to their wavelength, but all travel at 300,000km (186,000 miles) a second. Sunlight, including infrared radiation and ultraviolet light (UV), forms only 0.001 per cent of the range (spectrum) of the sun's e-m radiation. Although we call it 'white', it is actually colourless.

Starting with the highest energy and shortest waves (0.0001-nanometre wavelength – a nanometre, or nm, being one thousand-millionth of a metre) – and progressing to the lowest-energy and longest (over 10,000m or 32,810ft wavelength), the sun's e-m spectrum includes:

- Gamma rays
- X-rays
- Ultraviolet light
- Visible light – waves from 400 to 750nm that we perceive as red, orange, yellow, green, blue and violet
- Infrared rays, which provide heat
- Microwaves
- Television waves, radar
- Radio waves
- Very long waves, including power-frequency ones

Sunlight on Earth

Solar energy journeys through the vacuum of outer space to the Earth's atmosphere, which allows only visible light, infrared rays and some UV to pass through.

Why is the sky blue?

The atoms and molecules of the various gases, water droplets and particles in the atmosphere scatter those wavelengths of light we see as blue and violet in all directions, including into our eyes. So when we say the sky is blue, we mean the atmosphere is blue. It doesn't look violet because we see blue better.

If we were to travel as astronauts into outer space, the only things that could scatter sunlight's wavelengths would be our

The sun produces a wide spectrum of electromagnetic energy waves (opposite), but only infra-red rays, visible light and some ultraviolet rays penetrate the atmosphere to reach us here on Earth.

spacecraft, Earth and its moon, other planets, satellites, comets, space debris, and the clouds of subatomic particles called cosmic rays. Apart from these and the sun, we would see nothing; there would be no shadows, and outer space would be black, not blue.

What makes dawns and sunsets red?

Sunlight has a longer journey through the atmosphere at dawn than at other times of day as the Earth is curved. So the atmosphere's particles scatter the wavelengths we perceive as blue so much that they are filtered out, leaving only those which we see as red. As the day progresses, sunlight goes from red through pink, orange and yellow to white or even bluish at mid-day, when it's most intense. Then these changes in colour balance are reversed until sunset, when sunlight may again look red.

Rainbows

When white sunlight – sunlight with the full spectrum of light rays – meets rain in the atmosphere, the droplets bend waves of each wavelength by a different amount. This produces the rainbow's spectrum of colours.

While these are described as red, orange, yellow, green, blue, indigo and violet, indigo isn't there; Sir Isaac Newton added it in the seventeenth century to make the rainbow's six colours a more mystical seven!

invisible

visible

gamma rays
x-rays
ultraviolet
violet
blue
green
yellow
orange
red
infra-red
microwaves
TV and radar
radio waves
power-frequency electric waves

This surreal curtain of light is the aurora borealis, seen at night over a Canadian forest. The shimmering, flickering light comes from collisions between cosmic rays and atmospheric gases.

Moonlight

This is reflected sunlight. The moon orbits the Earth every 29.53 days, and its orbital position determines its 'phase'. If Earth blocks all its sunlight, we don't see the moon. If no sunlight is blocked, we see a full moon. And if some of the sunlight is blocked, we see a part of the moon.

Moonlight is beautiful and, according to legend, influences behaviour. When there's a full moon, researchers say that people tend to eat bigger meals, drink more and make more phone calls! Moonlight also increases the concentration of positive ions in the air, and there is some evidence that this makes blood stickier and encourages road-traffic accidents, aggressive behaviour, psychotic breakdown and epileptic seizures.

Firelight

Firelight comes from the energy released as molecules of a burning substance become progressively more excited. The hotter the fire, the shorter the wavelengths of light released. So a fire starts off red hot, then progresses through orange and yellow until it becomes white hot. The hottest part of a flame is the white part at the top.

Lightning

Swirling water droplets in clouds build up e-m energy. When this reaches a critical level, it discharges by travelling to Earth, at the speed of light, as a flash of lightning. The associated 30,000°C (54,000°F) of heat first expands then contracts surrounding air, causing a thunderclap that reverberates from nearby clouds. Around the world there are around 100 lightning flashes every minute; these produce some of the atmospheric ozone that protects us from too much UV.

Lightning can kill or damage by electrocution from its current of up to 250,000 amps, or by its intense magnetic field.

To protect yourself, inside:

● Stay off the phone

● Unplug the TV

● Ideally, avoid outside walls

Outside:

● Go inside; you are safe in a car

● Don't shelter under a tree, particularly if it's isolated or an oak

● Don't hold anything made of metal (including umbrellas and golf clubs) or carbon fibre (such as a fishing rod)

● Don't stand in a group

● If your hair stands on end, crouch in a ball with your feet together

Northern and southern lights

There are ethereal displays of swirling colours in the night sky. They result from the Earth's emf making cosmic rays – streams of electrically charged subatomic particles in the solar wind from outer space – spiral towards the poles. When these particles collide with molecules of gas in the Earth's ionosphere, the molecules become excited and release curtains of fluorescent light called the aurora borealis at the north pole, the aurora australis at the south.

Phosphors

These chemicals release coloured light when energized by UV or an electron beam. A television's phosphors release red, green and blue light. A fluorescent tube's phosphors create white light. A watch's luminous hands contain phosphors mixed with a radioactive element. Phosphors continue to release light for hours, as you can see from the 'glow-in-the-dark' stars some people stick to their bedroom ceiling.

The simple bare necessity of life

Light enables plants and animals to live and grow. Plants give humans, and other animals, a supply of vegetables, fruit, beans, grains, nuts and seeds, while animals provide us with foods such as fish, meat, milk, cheese, yoghurt and honey. Plants also provide fossil fuels for heating, cooking and industry. And plants and animals provide fibres such as cotton, linen, silk and wool.

Most important, plants help maintain the balance of oxygen and carbon dioxide in the air by photosynthesis, a chemical process involving light. A green pigment called chlorophyll in leaves traps the energy from sunlight. And it's fascinating that light doesn't have to shine on plants for this to happen; sunlight's energy can enable photosynthesis even when it's transmitted to a plant via a copper wire! Water and carbon dioxide interact with light's energy in leaves to form oxygen (for us to breathe) and carbohydrate (for us to eat).

Is light matter or energy?

For years scientists have debated whether light is matter, meaning it has 'mass', or whether it is purely energy. The answer, according to the latest thinking, is that it has some characteristics of both. Sometimes it helps to think of light as electromagnetic energy waves. At other times it's more appropriate to think of it as photons – a photon being a massless particle (one with no substance, or 'mass') or quantum of e-m energy.

Links with the body's energy system

Some light landing on the body is reflected straight off again. However, some enters the eyes, where it sends electrochemical messages to the brain, and some enters the skin. Some of this light entering the skin leaves fairly quickly. Some penetrates quite

A month in the life of a strong young shoot which breaks through the tough covering of a sessile oak tree (Quercus petraea) *acorn, then heads upwards, aided by heat and moisture and guided by sunlight.*

deeply, where it is mostly absorbed and converted into heat (which makes arteries and veins expand, increasing the supply of oxygenated blood to the area). Our cells also produce a minute amount of light.

Clearly, light is an active and important contributor to each person's energy, and the various wavelengths of light – which we perceive as different colours – have particular effects on us, too.

Light as a tool in 'energy medicine'

Not surprisingly, we can use light to influence the energy – and therefore the health – of the body as a whole, as well as of particular body systems. Some of the many ways we can do this are outlined in Part Two.

Teleportation

One fascinating new development involving light is the concept of teleportation – the instantaneous transport of information between two objects a long way apart. The technicalities are still in their infancy but scientists have already managed to engender teleportation by separating two identical photons. These then have a continuing and unbreakable relationship that enables information to travel instantaneously from one to the other. This technology may, in the foreseeable future, enable hugely powerful computing and microscopy.

Light's colour balance

The sunlight we receive doesn't contain the full spectrum of the wavelengths in the sunlight that enters the atmosphere. Its spectral or colour balance – the proportions of its various wavelengths – varies with the height of the sun in the sky, which depends on the season, latitude and time of day. It also depends on a place's altitude, and on the amount of cloud, mist or pollution. The shorter the distance sunlight travels through the atmosphere and the less cloud, mist or pollution there is, the bluer the light, and the further it goes through the atmosphere; the more cloud, mist or pollution, the redder it is. The colour balance of sunlight and other lights can also have important effects on our health and wellbeing.

Colours as 'vitamins' and light as 'food'

Light's wavelengths are absorbed differently by the blood's red pigment (haemoglobin), by the skin's brown pigment (melanin), by yellow bile pigments in the blood or skin, and by other coloured substances such as plant pigments like carotenes in our skin and eyes.

Haemoglobin travelling in red blood cells in the skin's blood vessels absorbs blue and green light, and reflects red light. Melanin, in cells called melanocytes, absorbs most light, especially towards the blue end of the spectrum, but is particularly good at absorbing UV.

The various wavelengths have other biological differences too. For example, blue light may be calming, and red stimulating. If a light's colour balance is lacking or over-represented in one particular colour, this can affect health. This is why some people say light's colours are like vitamins. We can take this analogy further with food and light in general, because just as we can have too little or too much food, so too can we suffer from light starvation or 'malillumination', or light overdose.

Depth of penetration by various colours

Light's various wavelengths penetrate the skin to very slightly different depths. The shorter the wavelength, the higher its energy and, perhaps unexpectedly, the less far that wavelength goes. So UV and blue light don't go in quite as far as red light or, for that matter, infrared.

One reason is that photons from higher-energy UV and blue waves excite charged particles called electrons in the skin more than longer wavelengths do. This means electrons 'play' with blue photons longer than with red ones. As a result, blue light bends more in the skin than red and orange light, and so doesn't travel as far.

All light's wavelengths except UV travel up to 3-4mm ($\frac{1}{8}$-$\frac{1}{7}$in) into the body, with the longest wavelength, red, going furthest. Indeed, very bright light can penetrate up to 7cm (2$\frac{1}{2}$in)! Normally, however, only around 1 per cent of blue light reaches much over 3mm ($\frac{1}{8}$in); 5 per cent of both green and orange light gets to 3.5mm ($\frac{1}{7}$in); and 21 per cent of red light goes to 4mm ($\frac{1}{6}$in). In contrast, only 20 per cent of UV's UVA fraction travels anywhere near 1mm ($\frac{1}{25}$in), and only 10 per cent of its UVB to 0.5mm ($\frac{1}{50}$in).

The upper block looks red because the ink absorbs every colour of light landing on it except red, which it reflects. Similarly, the lower block reflects only blue.

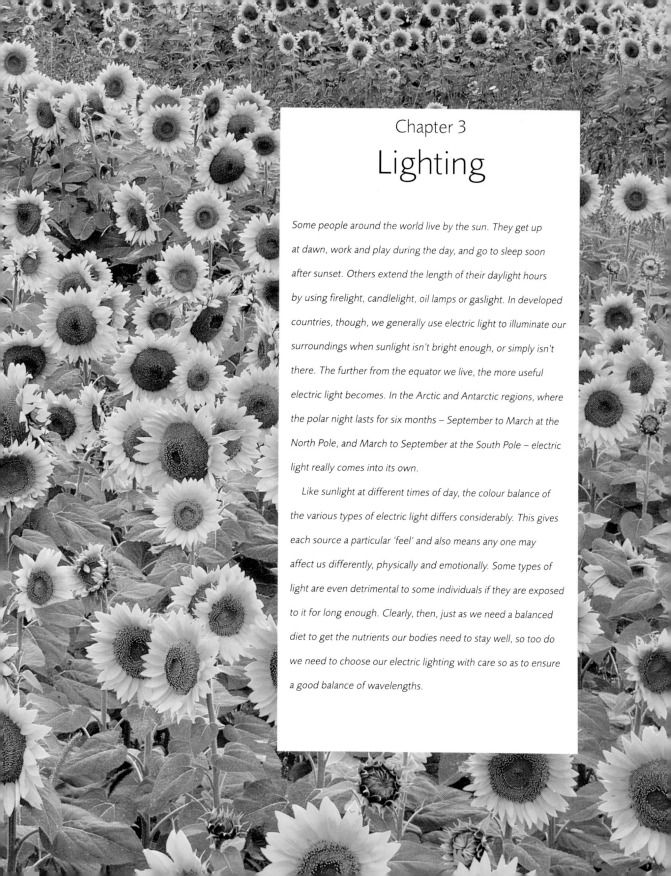

Chapter 3
Lighting

Some people around the world live by the sun. They get up at dawn, work and play during the day, and go to sleep soon after sunset. Others extend the length of their daylight hours by using firelight, candlelight, oil lamps or gaslight. In developed countries, though, we generally use electric light to illuminate our surroundings when sunlight isn't bright enough, or simply isn't there. The further from the equator we live, the more useful electric light becomes. In the Arctic and Antarctic regions, where the polar night lasts for six months – September to March at the North Pole, and March to September at the South Pole – electric light really comes into its own.

Like sunlight at different times of day, the colour balance of the various types of electric light differs considerably. This gives each source a particular 'feel' and also means any one may affect us differently, physically and emotionally. Some types of light are even detrimental to some individuals if they are exposed to it for long enough. Clearly, then, just as we need a balanced diet to get the nutrients our bodies need to stay well, so too do we need to choose our electric lighting with care so as to ensure a good balance of wavelengths.

Electric lighting

The decisions we make when choosing electric lighting are important for their practicality and visual appeal, and because they can influence our health and wellbeing.

Brightness

Bright light enables 'photopic' vision – the use of cones in the eye to see colour and fine detail. In extremely dim light we have only 'scotopic' vision, from our rods, meaning we see in shades of grey. So electric lighting enables us to see colours at night.

On a practical level, electric lighting is often important for safety, as falls and other accidents – and criminal attacks– are more common in the dark. This makes the planning of good lighting an important, if unsexy, concern for places such as streets, pathways, passages and flights of stairs.

People who don't get enough bright light are more prone to many common health problems, including depression, obesity, high blood pressure, arthritis, fertility problems, poor sleep, infection and cancer. Some of us go outdoors very little, and work in buildings with little natural daylight. Yet electric light alone is rarely bright enough to prevent light-deficiency disorders.

Measuring brightness in lux

Brightness is measured in lux, 1 lux equalling the light 1.5m (5ft) from a standard candle. Living-room lighting in the evening is around 100 lux; a well-lit kitchen or workplace is usually 300-500 (700 at most). As for outdoor daylight, twilight is around 100 lux, a rainy winter day around 2,000, a sunny spring morning 10,000, a bright summer's day 60,000, and a Mediterranean beach, 100,000.

Direction

Certain tasks, such as cooking, reading, writing and any craft work, are more

comfortable, easier and safer with directional 'task' or 'focal' lighting. This is often best when it comes from above, or from over the left shoulder. However, if you have an Anglepoise-style lamp you can put it on your desk and direct it at your work without its light shining in your eyes. Other activities, such as indoor sports, are fine with diffuse or background lighting.

Fitments

A fitment's light can be altered by a shade or filter. For example, a shade lined in white brightens light, while a coloured shade or filter alters its colour balance and a dimmer lets you adjust its intensity. The choice includes:

● Ceiling-fitted lights, dangling, flush or recessed. These can provide diffuse or directional lighting, including spotlighting, downlighting (with a down-pointing beam), and wallwashing (to flood a large area of wall with light).

● Wall-fitted lights. These provide localized diffuse lighting or directional lighting, including spotlighting, uplighting and downlighting.

● Stand-alone lights. These include table lights, clip-on lights and floor-standing lights, and can provide local or general diffuse lighting, or directional lighting, including spotlighting, uplighting and wallwashing.

● Specialist fitments. These include strips of light along stair-tread fronts; light boxes and visors for light therapy; lights worn on the head for working outside at night, night lights for young children's bedrooms; and 'dawn lights', whose intensity gradually increases to simulate dawn and wake a person gently.

Looking from a weather-forecasting satellite in outer space, it's possible to see towns and cities brightly lit by millions of electric lights, and areas of countryside that appear completely dark.

Tungsten-filament 'incandescent' light

Electricity makes a bulb's wire filament glow with white-hot heat, which gives 'warm' light with red and yellow predominating. Compared with daylight this light is relatively lacking in green, has even less blue and violet, and contains very little UV.

Fluorescent light

Electrically excited gas emits UV which makes phosphors fluoresce; the light's colour depends on the phosphors.

In light from cool-white tubes – the commonest sort – green and yellow predominate, and red and blue/violet are relatively lacking; warm-white tubes provide relatively more red. Standard fluorescent light contains very little UV, and adding a plastic diffuser blocks 17–99 per cent, depending on its material.

Full-spectrum fluorescent light has a much more natural colour balance, and without a diffuser – or with a UV-transparent diffuser – gives 10 per cent UV and 90 per cent visible light, which is similar to the proportions in sunlight. This UV can be good for people who spend a lot of time inside and get little outdoor daylight. It is extremely unlikely to be a health hazard since its intensity is vastly less than that of daylight's UV.

One researcher found that people had higher levels of stress hormones under standard fluorescent light, but not under full-spectrum fluorescent light. Other researchers noted more cancer in office workers under standard fluorescent light, and more fatigue, irritability, poor concentration and hyper-activity in children who spend a long time in this light. Standard tubes flicker (at 100–120 times a second) because the phosphors don't glow throughout each of an alternating current's energy cycles. While most of us don't consciously notice this, a few find it annoying; at worst it can cause headaches, eyestrain, nausea or epilepsy. Old or faulty tubes flicker more slowly, making problems worse. A tube which has an electronic ballast produces virtually flicker-free light.

Halogen light

Halogen gas makes a heated tungsten filament glow with cool light that has a more natural colour balance than that of most incandescent or fluorescent light. However, it emits

Tubes of coloured light bent into pictures, words and symbols, opposite, add to city-centre excitement at night, but only the red ones contain neon – the others contain krypton, argon or other gases.

proportionately more UV than sunlight, though of course the intensity is very much lower.

The low-voltage transformer needed to run a halogen light from a mains supply produces quite a strong emf that extends to 90cm (3ft) all around. Because of unproven health concerns, it's wise not to sit within this range. Halogen lamps also need a lot of space around them to dissipate their heat.

Colour balance of electric light

A light's 'colour temperature' is a way of describing its colour balance. That of daylight varies from below 2,000°K (Kelvin) at sunset, to 5,600°K for 'standard' daylight, and 30,000°K on a sunny day. That of full-spectrum electric light is 5,000–7,500°K; other types of electric light have lower colour temperatures. Light with a lot of red has a relatively lower colour temperature, and light with a lot of blue a relatively higher one.

Another way of describing colour balance is with the colour-rendering index (CRI). Sunlight has a CRI of 100, and any lighting with a CRI over 90 is called full-spectrum. Confusingly, 'daylight' bulbs don't produce full-spectrum light.

Choosing lighting

Dim electric light makes colours look more like they do under natural daylight when it's 'warm'; bright electric light makes colours look more as they do in mid-day daylight when it's 'cool'.

When choosing, consider using full-spectrum fluorescent tubes (see page 156) if you spend many hours a day in a room with little daylight, and don't get out much. This will help prevent ailments influenced by colour deficiencies.

Lighting to look your best

Careful lighting can enhance the colouring of a person's face, hair and clothing, disguise certain features and make the most of others. Tips to try:

● Choose white or pearl tungsten-filament bulbs to make light less harsh and not as likely to cast shadows.

● Avoid overhead lighting as this casts unflattering shadows on the face.

● Warm light may make skin look more attractive in dim light, and cool or full-spectrum light may be better in bright light.

● Skin with a blueish cast (which probably

General activities – a tungsten-filament bulb; or a full-spectrum fluorescent tube (for good colour balance).

Relaxing – a tungsten-filament bulb (for 'warm' light).

Close work – a tungsten-filament bulb; a halogen bulb (for better colour balance); or a full-spectrum source (for good colour balance).

Kitchen – a fluorescent tube (for even illumination), or a full-spectrum source (for good colour balance).

Indoor sports – a full-spectrum fluorescent tube (for even illumination and good colour balance).

looks better with white by it, not cream) may be most flattered with halogen or full-spectrum light. Skin with a golden glow (which probably looks better with cream by it, not white) may be more flattered by warm light.

● Cool-white fluorescent light is harsh and

Lighting a recess, niche or alcove is a simple but effective way of adding interest and focus to a room. Coloured light is even more dramatic.

sometimes called 'cruel' white; standard fluorescent light may have an unflattering pale yellow-green bias.

Feng shui

Feng shui – from the Chinese for 'wind and water' – is a method of optimizing the siting of buildings and the arrangement of their rooms to improve health and wellbeing. It is based on a combination of common sense and professional observation, but has a sprinkling of superstition and eastern mystical ideology.

Both the north/south/east/west positioning of a house and its rooms, and its lighting, are considered very important to the 'energy' and ambience of a building and each of its rooms. The various directions are believed to confer particular benefits on particular aspects of an inhabitant's life, health and aspirations. However, you can alter the ambience of a room not reckoned to be in the most favoured aspect by using one or more simple lighting techniques. These include:

● Putting a mirror in the dining room (to reflect people and increase a feeling of conviviality), but not in the bedroom (as gazing at yourself lying in bed could encourage introspection!).

● Hanging a crystal to reflect shafts of light, and rainbows (said to increase the 'energy' of a room).

● Making a dark hall lighter by installing mirrors or keeping lighting on (to foster a sense of welcome).

Chapter 4
Coloured light

Sunlight (or any other white light) is invisible. It's only when it lands on something that we see it. If the object reflects all the light, we see white light because our eyes receive all the wavelengths of the white light from the source. As a result, the object looks white. But if something reflects only some of the light's wavelengths, and absorbs energy photons from the others, we see only the reflected wavelengths. These determine the colour we perceive the object to be. For example, something that looks violet has absorbed the wavelengths of light we perceive as red, orange, yellow, green and blue, and reflects to our eyes only those we perceive as violet.

A black object absorbs all light's wavelengths, while something that's totally transparent allows them to pass right through. Coloured glass (and other coloured, semi-transparent materials) allows only certain wavelengths to pass through and absorbs the rest. Red glass, for example, absorbs violet, blue, green, yellow and orange rays, but allows red ones through.

Years of observation have taught scientists a lot about how colours affect the growth, health and behaviour of plants, insects, fish, lizards, birds and mice. Today we know quite a lot about how colour affects humans too.

How colour affects us

We can see at least 10 million different colours or 'hues'. These colours affect us in different ways, the major differences being between those at the blue and red ends of the spectrum. Overall, all light is stimulating. But violet and blue tend to be relatively less so, and red and orange relatively more so. This means, for example, that blue may relax a tense person.

However, a person's response is also based on their experiences and emotional associations with colours, and these may override other responses, so some people, for example, find red calming and blue stimulating. Also, red is most likely to excite people who already feel excited, overactive or aggressive, whereas blue is most likely to calm those who already feel calm and relaxed, since colour can exaggerate a person's existing state.

Whatever a person's physiological response, it won't last long and may be followed by the opposite. So red, for example, may initially be stimulating, but later become calming.

Interestingly, researchers say that exposure to strong stimuli – such as loud sounds, or strong smells and tastes – makes eyes more sensitive to green and less sensitive to red. The illegal psychoactive drugs mescaline and LSD can make colours supernaturally vivid. And certain conditions temporarily alter colour perception – for example, jaundice can make things look yellow; alcohol poisoning, blue; cataract removal, blue; and glaucoma and diabetic retinopathy, yellow.

What scientists say colour can do

Red
- Stimulates the sympathetic nervous system
- Excites
- Arouse interests
- Energizes
- Disturbs anxious people
- Warms
- Boosts skin and blood cell regeneration
- Enhances wound healing
- Improves circulation
- Increases reaction time
- Raises blood pressure
- Increases respiration rate
- Increases blinking frequency
- Normalizes an inwards squint

- Improves learning
- Makes some people overestimate time
- Encourages shaking In some people with Parkinson's disease

Orange
- Boosts appetite
- Encourages the sensation of warmth

Pink
- Soothes violent or anxious adults for a few hours, then makes some of them irritable
- Stimulates creativity and strength in children

Yellow
- Boosts alertness
- Aids learning
- Encourages nausea

Green
- Rests eyes, because unlike red and blue, green is naturally focused almost exactly on the retina.
- Makes people underestimate time

Blue
- Stimulates the parasympathetic nervous system
- Calms anxiety
- Relaxes tense muscles
- Encourages boredom
- Cools the body

- Makes people underestimate time
- Reduces respiration rate
- Lowers blood pressure
- Normalizes an outwards squint

For some people, certain colours ease acne, eczema, psoriasis, cold sores, poor night vision, eyestrain, 'computer eyes', anaemia, jaundice, migraine, dyslexia, epilepsy and, perhaps – though research is needed – Parkinson's disease (see Part Three). Other claims come from anecdotal experience.

Other claims

Red – boosts confidence, motivation, assertiveness, strength, energy, sexual arousal; attracts; warns; encourages aggression and hyperactivity.

Orange – energizes; encourages sociability, enthusiasm, optimism and appetite.

Pink – promotes peacefulness.

Yellow – cheers.

Green – can tranquillize, arouse, or, more usually, balance.

Blue – soothes; reduces inflammation; makes babies less active and reduces crying; can foster depression and withdrawal.

Violet – promotes creativity and study.

Adding and subtracting colours

When two wavelengths or 'colours' meet, we see light with a wavelength which is an average of the two. When green and red light are shone on a white background, for example, we see yellow; green and violet-blue produce turquoise; and red and violet-blue form a purplish magenta. But when 'complementary' colours are shone together, they make white light. Examples are warm red and turquoise-blue, green and magenta, and yellow and blue-violet. None of this applies to painting or printing, because mixing pigments produces different results.

Colours can also be subtracted from light. For example, when sunlight lands on something green, its blue and red wavelengths are absorbed and its green ones reflected. And if sunlight travels through a blue gel (transparent acetate sheet, available from theatrical, art and photographic supply shops), and the resulting blue light travels through a yellow gel, you get green light, because only green wavelengths pass through both.

Colour blindness

Some people have one of several types of colour blindness – or, better, deficiency. The commonest type, red-green, at worst makes red and green things look grey. Blue-yellow colour blindness is another possibility. A very few people see virtually no colour. And very occasionally emotional trauma makes a person blot out a colour.

Colour blindness can be a burden to school-children, for example, in geography or art. And colour-blind people may be barred from being a technician, doctor, electronics or tele-communications engineer, naval officer or pilot.

Colour therapies

Colour therapies have been around for centuries. The ancient Egyptians and Greeks, for example, constructed temples with domes of crystals that let particular colours into rooms used for healing, childbirth or meditation. Interest waned, but has been rekindled over the last few decades, and scientists can now explain some of the effects of light and colour in terms of their effects on the levels or balances of various hormones and neurotransmitters.

Chakra	Gland
Root	Adrenals
Sacral	Ovaries and
	testes
Solar plexus	Pancreas
Heart	Thymus
Throat	Thyroid
Third eye	Pituitary
Crown	Pineal

The many colour therapies (see Part Two) include shining coloured light – perhaps focused, polarized, laser or flashing, depending on needs – on the whole body, an unhealthy area, an acupuncture or reflexology point, or the eyes. Other therapies include wearing tinted spectacle lenses; eating brightly coloured food and drink; drinking water that's been 'solarized' (exposed to coloured sunlight); having crystal healing; and choosing flowers or Aura-soma bottles. Many have measurable success. While some are not scientifically validated, they are very unlikely to cause harm, as long as you see your doctor if symptoms continue or are serious or worrying, so you don't fail to spot a serious condition that has an effective medical treatment.

Some therapists use coloured light from a torch with a coloured filter or crystal to stimulate or calm a chakra they believe to be unbalanced. They may use red, orange or yellow to 'tonify' or stimulate, or green, blue or violet to 'disperse' or calm.

The box above gives a list of the chakras, with the endocrine (hormone-producing) glands traditionally associated with them.

The coloured circles illustrated here come from one of a set of ten cards – each with a different combination of colours – that are sometimes used to test for colour blindness.

Using colour in your home to affect your mood

The colour of indoor light depends on the colour balance of its daylight and electric light, and on its contents. Black (unless very shiny) absorbs all wavelengths, while white reflects all. So painting a ceiling white reflects all the source light.

Paint comes in a myriad of tints, tones and shades. A tint is a 'pure' colour mixed with white; a tone is a colour mixed with white and black; and a shade is a colour mixed with black. Hue is simply another word for colour.

When choosing colour schemes, ask yourself these questions:

Which colours do I really like?

Include your favourite colour, though you may not want much if it's a strong colour. The most popular colour with adults is blue, followed by red, green and violet and then, in men, orange followed by yellow, and in women, yellow followed by orange. Most people have stronger emotional reactions to brightness and vividness than to actual colour.

Would I like more stimulation or energy?

If so, consider choosing either 'warm' colours – hues, tints, tones and shades of red, orange or pink – and/or bright colours.

Would I like to feel calmer or more relaxed?

If so, consider choosing 'cool' colours – hues, tints, tones and shades of blue or blue-green, and avoid bright colours.

Do I sometimes want more stimulation, sometimes more calm?

If so, make walls, floors and ceiling neutral, and introduce flexibility with coloured rugs, cushions, throws, decorative objects, or lights (see panel opposite). Or go for green.

Will I be concentrating on close work?

If so, choose softer, cooler colours to avoid distraction.

What social activities do I want to enhance?

Warm colours are welcoming, encourage eating, and are good for socializing and partying; cool ones foster being quiet and 'chilling out' alone.

Do others use the room?

You can't suit everyone, so consider going neutral for walls, ceilings and floors, then introducing colour with paintings, books, flowers, etc.

See for yourself the difference warm and cool colours make to the 'feel' of a room, opposite, with the cooler, green tones inviting quiet pursuits and the warm ones more conviviality.

● Staple fabric scraps and small pieces of carpet on to white card, and add patches of paints to see if you like them together.

● A colour doesn't have to be bright or widespread. For example, having a touch of red in a neutral room can mean more, emotionally and symbolically, than having red walls.

● A little of your main colour's complementary colour (see page 42) can bring a room to life.

● Dragging or sponging one colour over another can be very attractive.

● Since the eye makes warm colours 'advance', use them for emphasis. Conversely, cool colours make things recede.

● Light, bright colours attract more attention than dark, subdued ones.

● Startling combinations include yellow/violet, orange/turquoise blue, and red/blueish-green.

● Vary colour effects by choosing surfaces with different textures and reflectancies.

● Experiment with coloured lampshades or bulbs, theatrical gels, or fluorescent-tube filters ('sleeves', see Coloured sleeves, page 156).

● Certain colours of light tend to dull or cancel their 'complementary' colour: for example, warm red cancels turquoise, magenta cancels green, and blue-violet cancels yellow, and vice versa.

The colour of clothes

One of the most rewarding things about selecting clothes is choosing their colours. But this can also be important in other ways. First, you may simply enjoy certain colours, or find them flattering. Second, looking at bright colours may, in very bright light, at least, influence hormone and neurotransmitter levels. And third, you are almost bound to have emotional associations with colours, based on past experiences, so you may have good reason to love or hate certain colours.

Sibling colours

When Annie, 33, was a girl of six, her mother bought her a dark red 'best' dress, thinking it would suit her dark hair and pale skin. But Annie preferred pink or powder blue, the colours chosen for her blonde, blue-eyed baby sister – the one who got all the attention. So she made a big fuss, even though she had to wear the red dress in the end. Not surprisingly, as a grown woman, Annie dismissed dark red as a flattering colour for many years. For although she had a rewarding career and family life, it made her uncomfortable. It wasn't until she and her younger sister discussed how she'd felt that she could begin to enjoy wearing dark red, and to own pink and powder blue as 'her' colours, not just her sister's.

Red for 'go'

Jules, 41, wore a new red suit for the final interview for her management-consultancy job. She was very nervous and knew the competition was stiff, but the interview went so well that she really enjoyed herself and felt she sparkled and gave her best. Jules landed the job. And since then she has always been able to rely on red when she needs a special confidence boost.

Emotional literacy and the colours you wear

Your reasons for choosing colours probably vary from day to day.

For example, you may choose a colour because:

● You like it

● Someone else likes it

● It represents how you feel

● It represents qualities you lack

● You want to portray a certain image

- It makes you stand out in a crowd
- It doesn't make you stand out
- It boosts your confidence
- It makes you look slim
- It's the only choice as nothing else is clean, suitable, or fits

All these reasons are perfectly valid but it may be useful to understand them. Indeed, being 'emotionally literate' about the colours you wear can help you get the best from your wardrobe. For example, if you simply love a colour, thinking why could enhance the pleasure it gives you each time you wear it. And if you've nothing else that's clean, suitable or fits properly, you and your wardrobe need some 'tlc' (tender loving care), perhaps with help from a friend or even an image consultant.

Some people say that their clothes' colours produce the following effects:

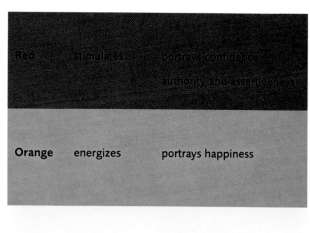

Red	stimulates	portrays confidence, authority and assertiveness
Orange	energizes	portrays happiness
Yellow	cheers	portrays light-heartedness
Green	soothes	portrays tranquillity and dependability
Blue	relaxes	portrays peacefulness and honesty
Violet	inspires	portrays creativity and thoughtfulness

Choosing colours to flatter your skin

Some artists use red, violet, blue, green and yellow amongst what we might think are normal skin tones when representing the skin. The light reflected by skin does indeed of the red pigment (haemoglobin) in the blood.

Given that our emotional and physical state, as well as our environment, can affect so many of these things, it's hardly surprising that our face can change in colour from

Does your skin have yellow in it?

1. Remove any make-up, clean your face, and fasten your hair back with a band or scarf. Position a mirror so your face is well illuminated by bright mid-day light. Then take a good, objective look to see whether there is any obvious yellow.

2. If you can't decide, ask a friend or relative for their opinion.

3. If neither of you can decide, get two large pieces of cloth, one white and one cream (a scarf or folded sheet will do, though whatever you use should be smooth, to reflect light evenly). Hold first one below your face, then the other. You'll almost certainly find that one of these colours brings your face to life very much more than the other. If it's the cream one, you probably have yellow tones in your skin.

Make-up comes in a myriad of tones and textures, opposite, all set for you to select the colours that suit your skin, flatter your eyes and hair, and help you feel your most attractive.

contain many colours. This is partly thanks to obvious things like its texture, thickness and pigmentation, the turnover of its cells, the amount of sweat and skin oil (sebum) on its surface, and the amount, type and colour of any make-up. But it's also thanks to the size of the blood vessels in the dermis (the deeper layer of skin), the rate of flow of the blood, the extracellular fluid and lymph, and the amount

season to season, let alone from month to month, day to day, and even hour to hour.

Having said all this, though, each person's skin colour has certain permanent definable colour characteristics. Perhaps the most important when choosing colours for clothing, make-up, jewellery and possibly even hair colour is whether it contains much in the way of yellow tones.

If your skin has yellow tones, then warm colours (such as russets, scarlet, bronze, orange, peach, ochre, yellows, cream, camel, beige and yellow-greens like olive and khaki) will probably suit you better for clothes and make-up than cool ones (such as violets, blueish-reds, taupe, blueish-greens and blueish-greys). And gold jewellery may look better on you than silver. If your skin lacks yellow tones, you may find that cool colours and silver jewellery are better. Most yellows are omitted from the warm-colour list, but a very pale lemon yellow may be fine, and you can always wear brighter yellows well away from your face.

This doesn't mean you can't wear every colour. The experience of make-up artists, hair stylists and image consultants suggests that everyone can wear every basic colour. We simply do ourselves a favour by choosing those hues, tints, tones and shades of each basic colour that suit us best.

The emotional and other symbolism of colour

Our use of colours as symbols is closely intertwined with our language, rituals and many other aspects of everyday life. In each country and every civilization, people have used colour to record their world and their emotions, to make rituals more meaningful, and to beautify celebrations. Many languages, for example, use expressions to describe emotional or physical states that include colour. We talk of 'seeing red' when we are angry, 'feeling blue' when we are depressed, being 'browned off' when we're fed up, being 'green with envy', and 'seeing the world through rose-tinted spectacles' when we're happy or in love. To some extent this may reflect the physical effects colour can have on us: while most people are excited by red, for example, it makes a few people feel genuinely aggressive. In contrast, light from the blue end of the spectrum is less stimulating, and for some people it's even depressing.

We speak of reds and oranges as 'warm' partly because they are the predominant colours in fire, and we speak of blues as 'cold' partly because of their association with the sea. But light from the blue and red ends of the spectrum may also have physical effects on our temperature. Although these effects are slight, red tends to speed the heart rate, which brings more blood to the skin and makes it feel warmer, while blue has a less pronounced stimulant effect, and compared with white light could be interpreted as being cold.

Many religions use colour to symbolize spiritual ideas and stages of spiritual growth. The Christian book of Revelation contains wondrous descriptions, involving colour and precious stones, of Christ's second coming; and the Hindu Ramayana contains similarly astounding descriptions of the 'other world'. Moslem men who have made their pilgrimage to Mecca wear green in their turbans in memory of the prophet Mohammed, and to signify they have made the journey. Western cultures often associate the devil with black, while Eastern cultures are more likely to make devils red. And a major part of the naming of white and black magic has to do with deep-rooted associations of white with sunshine, life and goodness, and black with night, death and darkness.

Red dresses are traditional for Chinese brides, opposite, and they certainly add an air of gaiety and passion that contrasts with the white ones – symbolizing virginity – favoured in Western Europe and North America.

Clothing

The use of various colours in celebrations and other rituals differs from country to country, and from one religion to another, because it is based on each colour's historical associations. If we look at wedding dresses, we see the favoured colour in westernized countries is usually white, because it is associated with virginity and purity, but wedding dresses in the East are often brightly coloured. In most European countries mourners traditionally wear black to symbolize sadness and loss, but in Turkey they may wear purple.

On this note, it's fascinating to look at the colours we choose for our clothes, because apart from choosing colours because they suit us, we may – perhaps quite unconsciously – choose them to symbolize important emotions or stages of life.

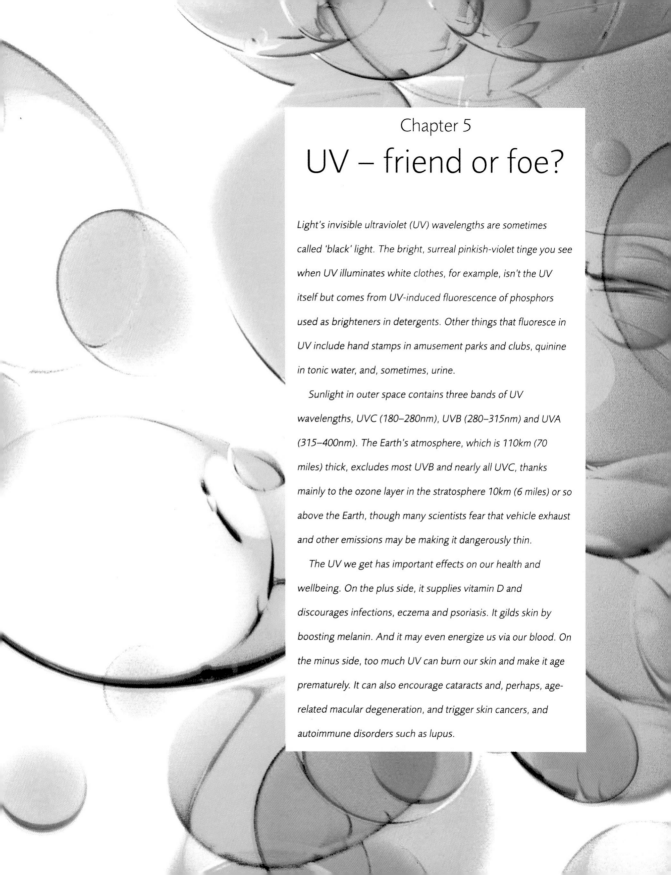

Chapter 5
UV – friend or foe?

Light's invisible ultraviolet (UV) wavelengths are sometimes called 'black' light. The bright, surreal pinkish-violet tinge you see when UV illuminates white clothes, for example, isn't the UV itself but comes from UV-induced fluorescence of phosphors used as brighteners in detergents. Other things that fluoresce in UV include hand stamps in amusement parks and clubs, quinine in tonic water, and, sometimes, urine.

Sunlight in outer space contains three bands of UV wavelengths, UVC (180–280nm), UVB (280–315nm) and UVA (315–400nm). The Earth's atmosphere, which is 110km (70 miles) thick, excludes most UVB and nearly all UVC, thanks mainly to the ozone layer in the stratosphere 10km (6 miles) or so above the Earth, though many scientists fear that vehicle exhaust and other emissions may be making it dangerously thin.

The UV we get has important effects on our health and wellbeing. On the plus side, it supplies vitamin D and discourages infections, eczema and psoriasis. It gilds skin by boosting melanin. And it may even energize us via our blood. On the minus side, too much UV can burn our skin and make it age prematurely. It can also encourage cataracts and, perhaps, age-related macular degeneration, and trigger skin cancers, and autoimmune disorders such as lupus.

Enough is enough

Skin tries to protect itself from too much sunlight by thickening and darkening, but tanned or naturally dark skin can still be damaged.

some UVA and 98 per cent of UVB, laminated glass blocks most UVA and all UVB, and UV-screening glass bars all UVA and UVB. Use this chart to estimate how long you can stay in the sun:

Your sunburn risk

Solar UV index	Skin-type 1 ('white', burns easily)	Skin-type 2 ('white', tans easily)	Skin-type 3 ('brown')	Skin-type 4 ('black')
1-2	Low	-	-	-
3-4	Medium	Low	-	-
5	High	Medium	Low	-
6	High	Medium	Medium	Low
7	Very high	High	Medium	Medium
8	Very high	High	Medium	Medium
9	Very high	High	Medium	Medium
10	Very high	High	High	Medium

Sunburn

This mainly results from UVB; the paler your skin and the more intense the UV, the faster you burn. UV intensity is greatest in summer, from 11am to 3pm, at high altitude, and in dry, clear air. Cloud reduces it by 20–40 per cent. Water, snow, sand and concrete reflect 80 per cent. UV can penetrate loose light clothing and 90cm (3ft) of water. Ordinary glass blocks

Note:

● The solar UV index (available on TV and in newspapers) indicates sunlight intensity.

● Type 1 skin is naturally 'white', and burns easily; type 2 is white and tans easily; type 3 is naturally brown; type 4 naturally 'black'.

● 'Low' risk means skin takes two hours or more to redden; 'medium' 1–2 hours; 'high', $1/2$–1 hour; 'very high', less than $1/2$ hour.

Premature ageing of the skin

UVA penetrates more deeply than UVB, producing free radicals that at worst can damage collagen, elastin and DNA. With limited exposure, the skin's antioxidants and enzymes mop up free radicals and reverse damage. But overexposure results in an accelerated ageing process called 'photoageing'. Its effects, most pronounced in fair skin, include:

● Lines, wrinkles, sagging and dryness.
● Age spots – freckles, red or skin-coloured lumps called solar keratoses, and rough, loose, yellow, brown or black greasy patches or lumps called seborrhoeic keratoses.

Skin cancers

Too much UV may encourage skin cancer:

● Malignant melanomas are uncommon but can kill if not promptly treated. They are 10 times commoner in white people and up to four times commoner in men. It's possible that regular, sensible sun exposure in temperate climates decreases the risk of melanomas by boosting vitamin D, but they are thought to be encouraged by occasional bursts of sun exposure at temperatures above 42°C (110°F), and by sunburn; they are most likely in fair-skinned people who burn easily.

● Non-melanoma cancers are slow growing and mostly affect fair skin that has been exposed to sun over many years. A rodent ulcer (basal cell carcinoma) starts as a pearly lump. Bowen's disease is a red scaly patch or lump with a one in 20 risk of becoming a slow-growing squamous-cell carcinoma.

Important: see a doctor for a cancer check if an 'age spot' or 'mole' darkens, enlarges, itches, reddens, bleeds, develops an irregular border, or ulcerates.

Sun rashes

The action of UV on light-sensitizing substances in the skin encourages photo-dermatitis (see pages 86–7); excess UVA encourages an itchy rash called polymorphic light eruption.

Eye damage

The cornea and lens absorb 99 per cent of UV, but over-exposure encourages cataracts and, perhaps, age-related macular degeneration.

Looking after skin in the sun

Skin goes on reddening for some hours after being in the sun. Aim to avoid even slight reddening, as this shows you have already had too much UV. There are many other ways of caring for your sun-exposed skin.

Food

Eating foods rich in omega-3 fatty acids helps suppress the particular balance of prostaglandins that encourages sunburn, and may help prevent skin cancer. And foods rich in antioxidants (beta-carotene and other plant pigments, vitamins C and E, selenium and zinc) help neutralize free radicals triggered by UV. Daily supplements of fish oil, beta-carotene and vitamin E may help too.

Clothes

Sunbathing, opposite, is popular with white people – the very ones it can damage most – so it pays for them to know how to look after their skin while enjoying the warmth and light.

One of the two most popular ways of limiting UV exposure is with clothes. The thicker and more tightly woven a material, the less UV goes through. White materials reflect most light, especially when brightened with fluorescent whitening agents. Some clothes are marked with a 'Clothing Protection Factor'

that indicates UV resistance (90 blocks 98 per cent of UV).

Shade

The second most common way is by staying inside or in a shaded place outside. In hot countries in high summer many people always avoid the mid-day sun.

Sunscreens

Most products claim to protect against UVB and UVA. The Sun Protection Factor (SPF) relates to UVB protection, and indicates how much longer it enables you to stay in the sun without burning. An SPF of 15, for example, indicates you can stay out 15 times as long. However, for this, sunscreen must be applied liberally and frequently – every hour or so – according to the instructions, replaced after swimming (unless waterproof) and towelling yourself dry, and not rubbed in.

Choose a product containing antioxidants such as beta-carotene, vitamins C and E, Pycnogenol or glutathione, as sunlight quickly exhausts the skin's natural supply of anti-oxidants. A special sun cream (ScalpBloc, see page 157) for bald heads is formulated to stay

on all day, and not make the scalp shiny or surrounding hair greasy.

There are several problems with sunscreens:

● Though they help prevent sunburn, age spots, and squamous cell carcinomas, there is no direct evidence that they prevent either rodent ulcers or melanomas.

● Most people use only $\frac{1}{4}$-$\frac{1}{2}$ the amount that gives the protection indicated by the SPF.

● Using the recommended amount is expensive; you might even need a bottle every day or two.

● Sunscreens don't block all UV and work only for a limited time. Many of us think too highly of sunscreens and therefore stay in the sun too long, which may increase our risk of melanoma.

● UVA protectors give skin a white sheen.

● Once opened, a sunscreen readily becomes infected, so a half-used one shouldn't be 'overwintered'.

● One UVA blocker, oxybenzone, is absorbed into the body. The long-term effects of this are not known.

● Sunscreens are less effective if you also use an insect repellent containing DEET.

● PABA (para-aminobenzoic acid) found in some products sometimes causes a rash; octyl methoxycinnamate may do so too.

Sand and light-coloured clothes reflect a high proportion of sunlight's UV rays, so take extra special care to protect a young child's skin on a seaside holiday.

Babies

Keep babies of up to six months out of direct sunshine, especially from 11am to 3pm – in summer in countries distant from the equator, and year-round near the equator – because their skin's melanin production is immature and they burn very easily. Use sunscreen only on an older baby's face or hands. Sunscreen isn't recommended for large areas because some ingredients may be absorbed and their long-term effects aren't clear.

Eyes and UV

Too much UV damages the eyes. If in bright sunlight between 11am and 3pm for long periods, wear a wide-brimmed hat or baseball cap, which halves the amount of UV entering the eyes, or wear UV-filtering sunglasses (see pages 94–6) or prescription glasses. Bare fluorescent tubes give off negligible UV, halogen lights a little more. People who particularly need to avoid UV (such as those with cataracts or photosensitive disorders) can fit a UV-blocking diffuser on a fluorescent tube.

It has been suggested, but not proved, that a little UV via the eyes may boost immunity, and actually encourage retina cells to regenerate.

Ordinary spectacle-lens plastic or glass blocks most UVB (and some UVA), sunglasses block even more, and UV-blocking lenses block it all. So until we know more, it may be wise not to wear glasses, contact lenses or sunglasses all the time outside.

Fake tan

Some people who want to look sun-kissed while avoiding too much UV use products that stain or otherwise colour the skin.

Treating sunburn

Have a long cool shower or bath, take an antioxidant supplement and smooth in an 'after-sun' product such as a moisturizer containing aloe gel or calendula, and antioxidants. If badly burnt, seek medical help.

Sunlight, UV and immunity – a plus or minus?

Sunlight – sometimes its UV in particular – affects our immunity, both locally in the skin (which is partly why it encourages skin cancer) and in the body as a whole. This can have good and bad effects. For example:

- Colds and other respiratory infections are less common in summer in countries well away from the equator.
- Skin infected by tuberculosis (TB) often responds well to sunlight's UV.
- In certain people, sunlight triggers attacks of autoimmune ('self-allergic') disorders such as lupus (see pages 151-2). Whether it does this via the eyes or skin – and if via the skin, whether or not UV is the culprit – isn't yet clear.
- The action of UV on certain sensitizers in the skin (see pages 86–7) can trigger light-sensitive allergic dermatitis.

Sex hormones

UV on the skin can boost the sex drive by raising the level of the sex hormone testosterone (present in women as well as in men). This helps explain why many people feel sexier during sunny holidays. Interestingly, research has found that UV shone directly on the scrotum raises a man's testosterone more than UV shone elsewhere.

Vitamin D production – a huge advantage of UV

UVB on the skin enables the production of vitamin D from cholesterol. This is a far more important source than our diet, and can provide 100 per cent of what we need.

Vitamin D is a hormone that affects many cells, for example those in the bones, brain, breasts, prostate, stomach, colon, pancreas, parathyroid glands, skin and bone marrow. A vitamin D deficiency due to a lack of sunlight is most likely in elderly people (as vitamin D production naturally falls with age); the housebound; dark-skinned people in very northerly or southerly latitudes; and middle-eastern women who wear long clothes and veils. Being overweight can make it worse. However, exposure of the face, hands and arms for a short time (five minutes for someone with type 2 skin, for example) two or three times a week in spring, summer and autumn produces plenty of vitamin D, with enough to last the winter. During the winter in northerly or southerly latitudes sunlight contains virtually no UV.

People who can't get enough sunlight on their skin need a vitamin D supplement, and

These Moslem women at prayer in Java have plenty of vitamin D, thanks to getting sunlight on their faces in a hot country, but if you cover up like this in a cool country you may need a supplement.

being on anticonvulsant drugs increases an individual's vitamin-D requirement.

Bones and muscles

Getting enough vitamin D prevents rickets in children, and osteomalacia and osteoporosis in adults; it also discourages muscle weakness and pain. UV increases physical performance, perhaps through the beneficial effects of vitamin D on muscles.

Teeth

Vitamin D helps prevent tooth decay.

Blood, blood vessels and heart

Vitamin D reduces high blood pressure for up to five or six days, and can lower cholesterol by nearly 13 per cent for 24 hours; this could make heart attacks less likely.

Blood sugar

Vitamin D can reduce insulin resistance ('pre-diabetes') and lower blood sugar. This can aid sugar-control in people with insulin resistance or diabetes.

Nerves

Low vitamin D production in very northerly or southerly countries is tentatively linked with a raised risk of multiple sclerosis.

Breast, ovary, prostate and colon cancer

Vitamin D helps regulate normal cell division and, perhaps, limit cancer-cell division. Researchers suspect that one reason the above cancers are more common in very northerly or southerly latitudes is a lack of sunlight-induced vitamin D. It's also possible that this may account for the raised risk of non-Hodgkin's lymphoma in these latitudes. Test-tube experiments suggest that vitamin D suppresses malignant melanoma and may encourage leukaemia cells to revert to normal.

UV as a disinfectant

Sterilizing water and blood

UV light has a disinfectant effect on water and blood (see page 102).

Cleaning air-conditioning systems

Bacteria and fungi here encourage respiratory infections in people who breathe the conditioned air, but irradiation with UV eliminates organisms within three weeks.

'Bioradiation'

Russian researchers claim that cells irradiated with UV radiate extra energy for some time. They also say that UV photons can energize haemoglobin in the blood as it flows through skin, and that this energized haemoglobin can boost the energy of other body cells. It has also been suggested that UV photons can energize the body via acupuncture meridians that act as fibre-optic 'channels' (see pages 98–9).

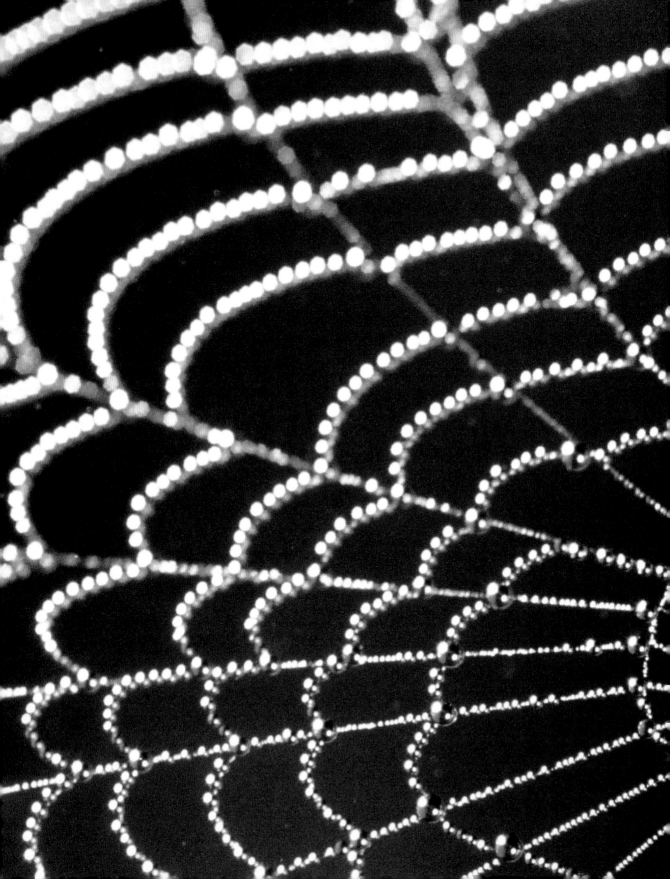

Chapter 6

Lighten your darkness

When we consider that the presence of the sun provides us with light and heat, and its absence with darkness and cold, it's hardly surprising that some ancient peoples worshipped the sun as a god. The three great monotheistic religions, Judaism, Christianity and Islam, don't have a sun god but their writings often describe their God in terms of light. In contrast, Buddhist enlightenment has nothing to do with a god or gods but with getting rid of an unhelpful reliance on earthly things.

Just as the sun and light are so often used as symbols of the divine, or of better understanding, so too have individual colours been used to represent aspects of the divine. And some people experience manifestations of light that they find extremely moving and describe as angels or the presence of God. Whatever our belief, each of us can learn to see each new day as a new beginning. One way of deepening our awareness of the divine, or of the beauty of creation – or simply of gaining a better understanding of our place in the scheme of things – is with a meditation involving light and colour. It's possible to use a visualization exercise for the same thing, or just to boost our spirits. There are guidelines on each of these later in this chapter.

The religious and spiritual significance of light and colour

Symbolic associations with light and darkness are present in many myths, stories and beliefs because sunlight is essential for life. Sunset symbolizes life's ending, while dawn suggests new life. This explains why the sun is a popular motif in every country, and why some cultures developed the concept of a sun god with power over darkness.

The Egyptians had Ra and Osiris; the Chaldeans Bel; the Babylonians, Marduk; the Indians, Surya and Brahma; the Greeks, Apollo and Helios; the Romans, Mithras; the Scandinavians, Woden (Odin); the Peruvians, Inti; the Aztecs, Huitzilopochtli, Tonatiuh, Tezcatlipoca, Tlalchitonatiuh and Yohualtonatiuh; the Mayans, Itzamna and Kinich Ahua; and the Japanese, Amaterasu.

Over the centuries many peoples continued to believe in a sun god, or to honour the sun, for example, at summer and winter solstice festivals. Even today, old beliefs linger in some people's concept of God living in the sky and in the pagan honouring of fire and light that finds echoes in the coloured lights on Christmas trees.

A menorah with the six-pointed star of David in the centre, opposite, and all the candles lit to commemorate the completion of the eight days of Hanukah (or Chanukah).

Judaism, Christianity and Islam

Light can represent wisdom, knowledge, justice and love, and symbolise the nature, experience or existence of the divine. The first chapter of the first book of the Bible, for example, says, 'And God said, "Let there be light," and there was light.' Then there are the rainbow of the Flood, Moses' burning bush, and angels – the messengers of spiritual darkness or light.

In John's gospel in the New Testament, John calls Jesus, 'The true light that gives light to every man'. A Christian's inner spiritual light is called 'the Christ light', and in Matthew's gospel, Jesus tells Christians they are 'the light of the world'. A star led the wise men and shepherds to the newborn Christ. And Christian saints are often portrayed with haloes.

The Talmud calls the presence of God the Shekhina and associates it with brilliant light. The Jews light Shabbat candles and, at Hanukah, the Dedication of Lights, they light one more oil wick or candle each day to commemorate how a tiny supply of oil miracu-lously burned for eight days after the temple was desecrated. The Jewish mystical tradition,

Kabala, teaches that everything is divine light in physical form.

The Koran says, 'God is the Light of the heavens and the Earth'. And when talking of different religions, the mystical Islamic tradition called Sufism says, 'The lamps are different, but the light is the same: it comes from beyond.'

Hinduism and Buddhism

A traditional oriental belief is that matter is made of concentrated light (which echoes the tenets of modern physics!). The word 'light' often expresses spiritual joy or riches. Buddhists say spiritual enlightenment – nirvana – is the acceptance that all things are one; their Festival of Lights ends with a procession of 1001 lights after dark. For Hindus, Krishna represents the light of wisdom, and people light lamps in their homes and temples at Diwali, the festival of thanks for the past and hope for the future, celebrating the triumph of light over darkness, good over evil.

Meditation with light and colour

Meditation helps many people develop greater spiritual understanding. Depending on their beliefs, it can enhance prayer or be a step to what Buddhists call enlightenment. At a provable biological level, meditation increases the brain's blood flow, enhancing creativity and alertness, and deeply relaxes the body. More mundanely, regular meditation encourages inner tranquillity and peace, and can ease pain and stress-related conditions – helping, for example, to lower high blood pressure and overcome insomnia. Light and colour are tried and tested aids to meditation, and can replace a mantra – a word repeated over and again to focus the mind. Some people like to focus on the flickering light from a fire or a candle flame, or a colour in a flower or painting. Others prefer being outdoors and watching the dawn, for example, or dappled sunlight beneath trees.

The following guidelines use colour to involve each part of your body while you are calming your mind.

Light one or more candles, opposite, to help you focus your mind and let extraneous thoughts float away as you meditate, or as you remember the life of a loved one now departed.

A colour-breathing meditation

● **Getting ready**. Find a time when you will be undisturbed for at least 20 minutes. Once practised, you'll find you can switch into meditative mode for a few minutes any time, however busy, noisy or uncomfortable your surroundings. Wear comfortable clothing and flat shoes (or none). The aim when learning is to have no physical distractions. Choose a quiet place that's neither too hot nor too cold. Sit on a firm, upright chair, legs uncrossed, feet flat on the ground, your back straight and resting against the chair's back. Your arms and shoulders should be relaxed, hands resting palms upward, in your lap.

● **Making a start**. Take a deep breath in and out, letting your abdomen rise and fall. This 'belly' breathing means your diaphragm is being well exercised, and you aren't restricting respiration by tensing your chest and your abdominal and back muscles. Continue with belly breathing, making each breath normal and rhythmical. Let any worrying thoughts float away. If at any time you feel faint or panicky, start yawning, or have pins and needles in fingers or toes, you are breathing too rapidly and getting rid of too

much carbon dioxide, which means your tissues aren't receiving enough oxygen.

● **Dedication**. Dedicate your meditation to God, or to 'good'.

● **Colour breathing**. Close your eyes and focus in your mind's eye on seven parts of your body (corresponding to the seven chakras), one by one (see below). For each, imagine the air around you flooded with light of the colour indicated. As you continue with your rhythmical belly breathing, imagine you are inhaling this coloured air. Continue with each colour for at least 10 breaths, going on for longer with any part that needs healing.

● **Afterwards**. Open your eyes when you are ready to 'return to the world'.

Bottom of the tailbone	Red
Top of cleft between buttocks	Orange
Umbilicus	Yellow
Centre of the chest	Green
Adam's apple	Blue
Centre of the skull	Indigo
Top of the head	Violet
Whole body	White

Imagining or 'visualizing' light and colour

Visual imagination – the creation of mind pictures with light and colour – can help heal the body, mind and spirit in two ways. First, the symbolism of its images, the intensity of the imagined light, and the colours we see can be emotionally or spiritually significant.

mimic the effects of bright or coloured light actually shone on the body.

We all benefit from imagining light and colour when we access memorised images we find spiritually enriching. Such images can act as icons to focus our mind on beauty, love and the meaning of life at any time. And they can be especially helpful when times are tough.

Visiting a magical garden

Step outside, through a doorway, into a garden. Your bare feet feel the cool moisture on the grass, and at the end of the long lawn sparkling with dewdrops you see the flush of dawn meeting the morning star. Slowly it brightens the sky with streaks of purple, aqua, lemon and orange light. It is the start of a new day, the first day of the rest of your life. You are aware the garden is for you, and you are very welcome.

Stretching out your arms, and raising them above your head, inhale the crystal-clear air deep into your lungs. Sense its freshness and energy permeating your body, into your pelvis, right to the tips of your toes and fingers, and into every part of your face – your lips, tongue, eyes, nose and ears – before it permeates your head.

Now walk on down the garden, and imagine yourself enfolded in the new sun's glowing golden light. Let your heart sing, if it will, with hope, or simply be aware that the garden will hold the hope for you until you are ready for it again. For you – (say your name) – are a child of the universe, a child of God. And as the daylight unfolds and the sky turns to blue, you know, deep in your soul, that all will be well ... and all will be well ... and all manner of things will be well.

Second, the mind's power and creativity can provably affect various neurotransmitters, hormones, 'feel-good' endorphins, and immune system factors. So it's possible, though not proven, that visualizing could

Some other ideas

● Make time for a daily 10–20 minute imagination or visualization session to think of scenes, people or things you love.

● If unwell, imagine your healthy cells

energizing and healing unhealthy ones.

● Incorporate visualization in your prayer, imagining, perhaps, that you can see God and that He or She is giving you the love and encouragement you need.

● When stressed, imagine overcoming a challenge that has been concerning you.

● Slowly read the box opposite and visualize and enjoy each sentence, or record it so you can listen to it at leisure. Even better, record your own material, filling it with light and colour, as your own aid to a relaxing and inspiring imagination session.

Chapter 7

How light and darkness affect what matters most

Light and darkness affect our mood, energy, sexuality, fertilty,
weight and lifespan. When we get enough light we're more likely
to feel well, happy, and full of energy. For bright light enables the
hypothalamus and the pituitary and pineal glands to help balance
our hormones and neurotransmitters. It also encourages good
sleep and a healthy weight. But too little bright light may make us
dull and lethargic. Life loses its sparkle and everything seems
hard. We get depressed, put on weight and go off sex.

So would it make sense to be exposed to bright light all the
time, day and night? The answer is no. For one thing, sleep
would be difficult, if not impossible, and for another, we actively
need darkness. Without it our pineal can't do its job of
converting serotonin – made when we're exposed to bright light
– to another substance that's very important to us, melatonin.
Daily exposure to bright light also helps set more than 100 of
our natural body rhythms to a 24-hour cycle, so we feel energetic
and sleepy at the right times of day, for example. So not only do
we need enough light and darkness, but we also need it in a
regular pattern if we're to feel our best.

Darkness and light

Our language is full of symbolic references to light and dark; we talk, for example, of 'light at the end of the tunnel'; of feeling 'bright', 'dull', or 'under a black cloud'; of 'lightening up' or being 'kept in the dark'. Indeed, it would be easy to think that brightness is inherently good and darkness inherently bad, but this isn't true. And it most certainly isn't the case with physical darkness and light because just as we need daily exposure to bright light, so too do we need daily darkness.

Serotonin and melatonin – messengers of light and darkness

The pineal gland is the body's light meter. Light stimulates it to make serotonin, and a lack of light stimulates it to make melatonin. Both these substances influence every body cell.

To make serotonin, the pineal modifies tryptophan, an amino acid from the blood. Serotonin helps prevent us from over-eating and boosts our feel-good factor, which is partly why people often feel happier in sunshine. Indeed, the best-selling modern antidepressant drugs are the SSRIs – selective serotonin reuptake inhibitors such as Prozac – that make serotonin more available.

As daylight dims, the pineal produces less serotonin. Once darkness falls, it stops releasing serotonin and instead produces a hormone called melatonin, made by modifying serotonin. Melatonin production generally peaks around 2–4am, when the amount in the blood is up to 10 times as high as during the day; we make from 5 to 25 micrograms each night.

At dawn, light tells the pineal to begin to stop making melatonin and begin to start releasing serotonin instead; as daylight brightens, we produce more and more.

Melatonin production stops almost completely when the light level goes above 2000–3000 lux (very bright light), and falls with only 200–300 lux (dim light). Blue and green light suppress melatonin production most effectively, while red and yellow do nothing. This means that incandescent electric light doesn't suppress melatonin as well as full-spectrum electric light.

Various other factors can also suppress melatonin production. They include drinking too much coffee or alcohol, smoking, and taking vitamin B12, beta-blockers or calcium-

This is a book about light, but darkness is vitally important too – for just as we need light, so we need darkness to keep our body chemistry working properly and help us feel well in body, mind and spirit.

channel blockers (for high blood pressure), diazepam, SSRI (selective-serotonin reuptake,) antidepressants, or non-steroidal anti-inflammatory drugs. Likewise, exposure to a marked extra-low-frequency emf (electromagnetic field), perhaps from faulty domestic wiring, reduces melatonin production.

Melatonin has many actions, and scientific evidence shows it is extremely important to our health and wellbeing. For example, melatonin:

● Helps control biorhythms such as the sleep/wake cycle, by controlling our body clock.

● Makes us sleepy and lowers body temperature and blood pressure.

● Affects the reproductive system and adrenal glands, influencing sexuality, fertility and stress.

● Boosts immunity.

● Acts as the body's most powerful antioxidant, which may help prevent age spots, certain cancers, heart attacks and strokes, and several other disorders.

Newborn babies make virtually no melatonin for three months, which helps explain why they don't sleep all night. And at the other end of life we make less melatonin, so someone of 60, for example, produces only half what they did at 20.

Melatonin is available as a supplement (see page 156) and in tests has given good results in the prevention of jet-lag; small studies suggest it may also help sleep problems. There is insufficient evidence to warrant using it for anything else.

Our body clock

The hypothalamus has a pinhead-sized 'body clock' that varies the levels of many hormones, enzymes and neurotransmitters according to the time of day or night. This body clock influences around 200 processes, including those that affect energy, hunger, blood pressure, body temperature, digestion, physical strength, reaction times, sexual appetite, urine production and brain power. It also affects our response to certain medications, and the timing of certain symptoms, such as arthritis pain. We may, for example, have early morning and late-afternoon peaks of energy and alertness, and be at our strongest physically from 4–7pm. Exposure to normal day-night cycles sets – or 'entrains' – the body clock to a 24-hour rhythm, and bright light is by far the most powerful entrainer.

The astronaut opposite is floating free, propelled by small, hand-held nitrogen thrusters, but when he is back in his spacecraft, orbiting Earth, he'll be crossing time zones so fast that he risks colossal jet-lag.

Owls and larks

Some of us are 'owls' – we feel at our best in the evening and prefer to go to bed late. But those of us who are 'larks' feel brightest and most alert in the morning. However, whether we are owls or larks by nature, getting up very late, perhaps not opening the curtains until mid-day and then using only dim electric light, inevitably reduces daylight exposure. On the other hand, getting up and going outside to work at dawn increases daylight exposure.

When the body clock goes wrong

When a person's body clock isn't working, their body's daily rhythms, or 'biorhythms', naturally fall into a cycle of 24 hours 11 minutes. Without other cues to entrain their body clock, this can be a real nuisance. It means, for example, that a person feels ready to wake up later each day, so that their preferred sleeping times are almost always out of kilter with those of other people.

Body clock disruption can happen to people who live in very northerly or southerly countries, where 'day' and 'night' last for months. It also happens in up to one in two people who are completely blind, depending, perhaps, on whether their optic nerves contain any fibres that can transmit messages about external light to the pineal, and whether they get any light on their skin.

Various situations may mean that body rhythms continue in their 24-hour cycle, yet

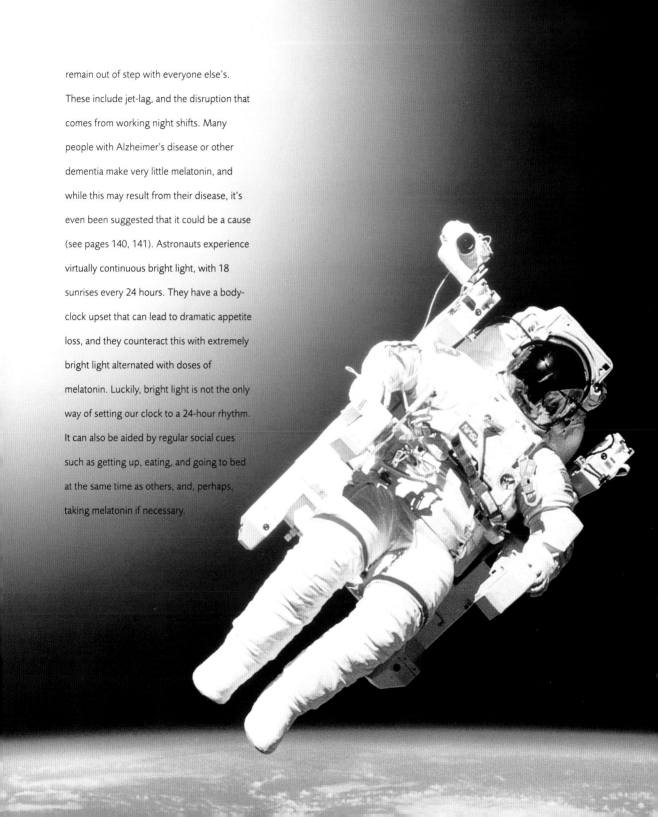

remain out of step with everyone else's. These include jet-lag, and the disruption that comes from working night shifts. Many people with Alzheimer's disease or other dementia make very little melatonin, and while this may result from their disease, it's even been suggested that it could be a cause (see pages 140, 141). Astronauts experience virtually continuous bright light, with 18 sunrises every 24 hours. They have a body-clock upset that can lead to dramatic appetite loss, and they counteract this with extremely bright light alternated with doses of melatonin. Luckily, bright light is not the only way of setting our clock to a 24-hour rhythm. It can also be aided by regular social cues such as getting up, eating, and going to bed at the same time as others, and, perhaps, taking melatonin if necessary.

Summer highs and winter lows

Many people feel at their best in the summer. One very likely reason is that they have higher levels of 'feel-good' serotonin produced by more bright light, though there are other possibilities, such as preferring warmer weather or liking summer holidays. Winter light is much less bright. And while it's possible to make up for this to some extent by using electric lights indoors, these are not usually bright enough to mimic bright daylight's effects on our hormones and neurotransmitters. Most of us cope very well with the relative dullness of winter days, even though some of us get only a little exposure to daylight because we are inside most of the time. However, some of us feel distinctly under par or get depressed. Scientists think one possible reason is a lack of bright light.

Winter depression

As winter draws on, around one in five people in the UK, for example, begin to be less well. They feel tired, heavy and fed up, and spring seems a long way off. In other words, they have the winter blues. Any of the usual causes of depression may occur in winter, but there are several reasons why winter itself can have this effect.

First, the weather could be to blame by discouraging us from taking exercise. When it's raining, foggy or freezing it's difficult to work up much enthusiasm to brave the elements and go for a walk. Yet more exercise would boost our circulation, allowing us to think more clearly and put problems in perspective. It would also increase our levels of 'feel-good' endorphins.

Second, a traditional winter diet may make us feel less than our best. A lack of fresh vegetables and fruit, along with too much fatty, stodgy food, could trigger digestive problems, bloating, heavy periods, poor resistance to infection and a lack of energy, all of which sap vitality. If this is the case, a better balanced diet could work wonders. Finally, a lack of bright light due to the low intensity of winter sunlight may cause a hormone imbalance, disturb the way the brain responds to serotonin, and upset the body clock.

The early-morning or late-afternoon light the workers opposite are getting as they go to or from work may not be enough to prevent ill health due to light deficiency – so hopefully they go outside at lunch-time.

SAD

Up to 3 per cent of people, more women than men, suffer badly from light-deficiency depression in winter, and are said to have seasonal affective disorder (SAD). Strictly speaking, this should be called 'winter SAD', because researchers have also identified a summer seasonal affective disorder. Someone with SAD may:

● Feel depressed, irritable and exhausted

● Crave sugary, starchy food (which boosts serotonin and may be the body's way of counteracting a lack of serotonin)

● Gain weight

● Feel cold

● Be abnormally tired

● Sleep badly

● Lose interest in sex

● Have lowered immunity

● Have painful joints

● Be temporarily overactive when light intensity increases in the spring.

The good news is that we can overcome SAD or 'winter blues' by, for example, getting more bright light (see page 139).

Sexuality and fertility

Our daily exposure to bright light and darkness has such far-reaching effects on our hormones that it's not surprising it can influence sexuality and fertility and generally keep our hormone balance in line. In fact, many people feel sexier in summer, when the light is brighter. One possible reason is that the opportunity to relax during a summer holiday boosts our interest in sex. However, research shows that sunshine (or UV alone) boosts testosterone. Sunlight exerts some its testosterone-boosting effect via the skin, and some via the eyes. Testosterone increases sexual interest and performance in men, and is certainly present in men in much higher levels than in women, but it is also important for sexual desire in women. Exposure to bright light also raises the body's levels of oestrogens, and one of the jobs these hormones do is help produce the moisture that lubricates the vagina during sex.

The amount of light affects sperm production and a woman's ability to conceive; a lack of light – which affects the melatonin level – makes people become less fertile. Eskimo women, for example, may stop having periods during the long arctic night. And people who live in very northerly countries are more likely to conceive in the spring, when light intensity increases.

Hormone balance

Because light stimulates the hypothalamus and the pituitary gland, it can influence the level of almost every hormone in the body. A lot of research remains to be done to see whether conditions such as an underactive thyroid gland might respond to treatment with bright light. However, it is certainly worth trying as a natural and non-damaging way of correcting any hormone imbalances connected with the pre-menstrual syndrome, polycystic ovaries and difficulties in conceiving.

Longevity, heart attacks and cancer

Several researchers suspect that having a healthy melatonin level could help prevent premature death. One reason is that melatonin is one of our most powerful natural antioxidants. This means it helps 'mop up' free radicals – active oxygen particles composed of 'singlet' oxygen atoms that have lost their

It's wonderful seeing bright daylight from the glass dome of Canary Wharf's magnificent new underground station in London – for we humans simply aren't programmed to stay underground for long.

partners. It's perfectly normal for the body to produce free radicals in response to physical stresses such as smoking, too much sunlight on the skin or too much exercise. But free radicals can cause trouble if not promptly mopped up because the body doesn't have enough antioxidant power from substances such as melatonin, beta-carotene and other plant pigments, vitamins C and E, selenium, zinc and superoxide dismutase. There might, for example, be a dangerous altering (oxidation) of low-density lipoprotein cholesterol in artery walls, making a heart attack or stroke more likely. Or it might encourage cancer.

Interestingly, women with oestrogen-dependent breast cancer tend to have a low melatonin level, as do men with testosterone-dependent prostate cancer. Bright light is needed to make the serotonin which, in turn, is needed by the pineal for melatonin production. So it's possible that getting too little bright light during the day could encourage these cancers.

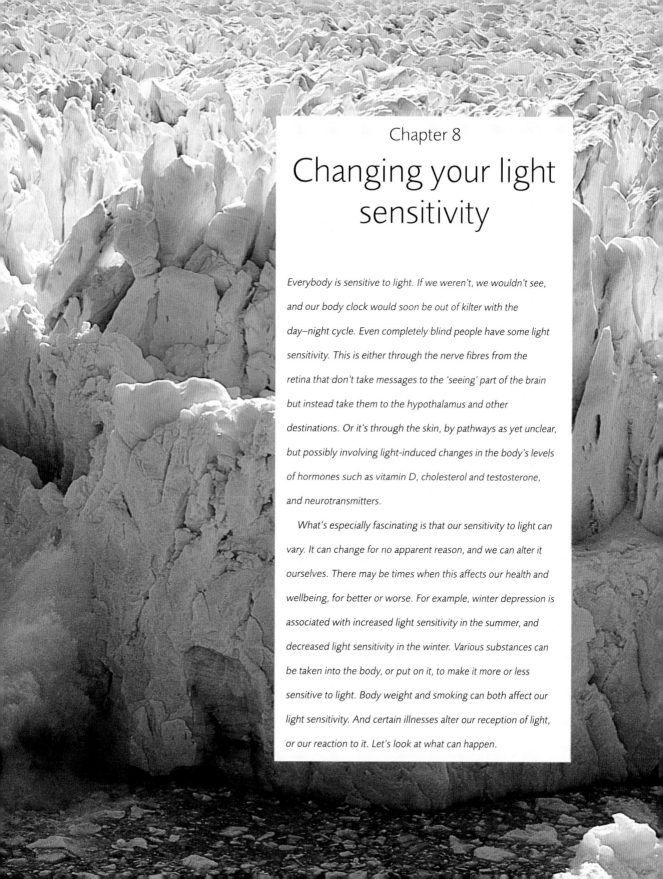

Chapter 8
Changing your light sensitivity

Everybody is sensitive to light. If we weren't, we wouldn't see, and our body clock would soon be out of kilter with the day–night cycle. Even completely blind people have some light sensitivity. This is either through the nerve fibres from the retina that don't take messages to the 'seeing' part of the brain but instead take them to the hypothalamus and other destinations. Or it's through the skin, by pathways as yet unclear, but possibly involving light-induced changes in the body's levels of hormones such as vitamin D, cholesterol and testosterone, and neurotransmitters.

What's especially fascinating is that our sensitivity to light can vary. It can change for no apparent reason, and we can alter it ourselves. There may be times when this affects our health and wellbeing, for better or worse. For example, winter depression is associated with increased light sensitivity in the summer, and decreased light sensitivity in the winter. Various substances can be taken into the body, or put on it, to make it more or less sensitive to light. Body weight and smoking can both affect our light sensitivity. And certain illnesses alter our reception of light, or our reaction to it. Let's look at what can happen.

Suntans and sunscreens

A suntan makes skin less sensitive to UV. Sunscreening products alter the colour balance of the sunlight that gets into our skin, effectively making us less sensitive to UV.

Antioxidants

These make us less sensitive to light by neutralizing potentially damaging particles called free radicals, produced by overexposure of skin and eyes to UV. We get some antioxidants from food, and make others in our body. We can also take antioxidants as supplements. Dietary antioxidants include vitamin A (for food sources, see page 119), beta-carotene, vitamins C and E, selenium, zinc and plant pigments (see pages 108–109). Melatonin is a powerful antioxidant made at night. However, its level falls if we get insufficient bright light during the day. Certain other things (see pages 72–3) can also influence it.

Eating a lot of parsley, opposite, or other foods that contain light-sensitive psoralens may increase the healing effects of sunlight's UV on the skin in some people with eczema or psoriasis.

Tryptophan

Some people develop SAD in summer if their diet lacks tryptophan. This rapidly lowers their brain's serotonin level, which is interesting because a good response to treatment with bright light for SAD depends on the brain having enough serotonin (as well as enough of two other neurotransmitters, noradrenaline and dopamine). To help ensure your body has enough tryptophan to make the serotonin and melatonin it needs, you should eat:

● Baked potatoes, bread, beans, hazelnuts, pumpkin seeds, dates, bananas and honey

● Enough fat, because having too little reduces the cholesterol level so much that brain cells can't use serotonin properly.

Body weight

Overweight people are particularly likely to eat an unhealthy diet that is short of fruit and vegetables and other sources of antioxidants. Also, because their portions of healthy meals may be too small to satisfy their needs, they top up their food intake with refined fatty, sugary and starchy foods that lack antioxidants. All this is a problem because a lack of antioxidants may mean that free radicals in the eyes and skin, caused by overexposure to UV, aren't mopped up well enough. This could encourage sunburn, premature ageing of the skin, skin cancer, cataracts and, perhaps, age-related macular degeneration. So if you are overweight, help protect yourself by eating healthy, satisfying meals and avoiding refined snacks.

Smoking

Both smoking and overexposure to UV increase the production of free radicals in the skin and eyes. This can encourage the same conditions as those suffered by overweight people with unhealthy diets – sunburn, premature ageing of the skin, skin cancers, cataracts and, perhaps, age-related macular degeneration. So becoming a non-smoker is an excellent way of helping to protect yourself against too much UV.

PUVA therapy

In this medical treatment you take a light-sensitive drug – a psoralen – which is distributed by your blood to all your cells, including those in the skin. When light-sensitized skin is then exposed to UVA light, the drug enables the skin cells to absorb more photons of UVA. This can be used to calm eczema and psoriasis, and increase skin pigmentation in people with white patches of vitiligo.

We can mimic some of the healing effects of 'medical' PUVA by eating foods containing natural psoralens (see pages 92–3), and then getting some sunlight on our skin. Remember, though, that psoralens will make you burn faster.

Hormone interactions

While a lack of bright light can trigger winter depression, and bright light can help prevent its symptoms, it isn't the cause. This is more likely to be a relative insensitivity of the brain to light in winter, though researchers aren't sure. Another possibility is that the body clock is disturbed in winter because it doesn't receive enough serotonin. Studies suggest that boosting serotonin in someone with SAD produces a weaker than normal surge of prolactin, cortisol, noradrenaline and growth hormone. This means these people are relatively insensitive to serotonin. One way of counteracting this is by stimulating higher levels with exposure to bright light. Others include taking the herbal remedy St John's wort, or an SSRI antidepressant drug, both of which can help the body respond to serotonin.

Eye disorders, glasses and contact lenses

Our sensitivity to light is reduced by any disorder that prevents light stimulating the retina, or prevents messages about light being

brain. Such disorders include short, long and far sight, cataracts, age-related macular degeneration, poor night vision, a detached retina and an inherited abnormality called retinitis pigmentosa.

Some children lose light sensitivity in one eye because they have a 'squint' (strabismus, or one or two 'crossed' eyes) and their eyes don't work in unison, or because one eye's vision is much worse than the other's. Either way, the vision from one eye may be blotted out – a condition called amblyopia. Sight can also be lost, or the visual fields dramatically reduced in size, after a traumatic event. Treatments involving light include stopping light from entering the eye that has good sight (for a squint), and stimulating the eye (or eyes) with poor vision with rapidly flashing light or coloured light. Finally, in a sense, glasses or contact lenses improve our sensitivity to light by enabling clearer vision.

White and coloured light

The major factor in the brain's sensitivity to light is the light's intensity, and this is true whether the light is white or coloured.

Moving, coloured, UV and strobe lights help give the club scene its unique appeal, but people with flicker-sensitive migraine or epilepsy may need to stay well away from particular effects (see Chapter 4, and pages 96–7). So if we colour white light by removing some of its wavelengths, we alter our sensitivity to light.

Flashing (flickering/pulsing/ strobing) light

The eyes and brain are particularly sensitive to flashing light. Flashing can be relaxing and healing (see pages 104–105), or alter our state of consciousness; and sometimes it's a health hazard. We don't consciously notice flashing that's faster than 30 or 40 times a second, but we readily notice if it's slower. A person's flicker-sensitivity depends on their age, and on a light's brightness, colour and angle. Sudden bright light increases adrenaline, a stress hormone, and flashing gives some people a headache, migraine or fit. Standard fluorescent lights flash 100–120 times a second, while an ageing tube may flicker more slowly. Modern TVs and computer screens emit flickering blue light, but the flashing is so rapid that it's unlikely to cause problems.

Light-sensitizing therapy

There are several sorts of photodynamic therapy (pages 104–105) that work by making the skin more sensitive to UV.

Light-sensitive disorders

Bright sunlight can trigger a blistering rash called solar urticaria ('nettle rash'). It can also trigger certain autoimmune disorders (see Lupus, pages 151–2, polymorphic light eruption (page 117), a blistering condition called pemphigus, and cold sores (page 112). It can create pigmented patches of melasma, (page 116), encourage cataracts (pages 121–2) and worsen rosacea (page 115) and several rare inherited disorders, such as phenylketonuria, porphyria and xeroderma pigmentosum.

Many illnesses can be triggered by a lack of light – for example, depression (pages 139–140) and fertility problems (pages 137–8). And a large number of problems, many mentioned in Part Three, respond to treatment with light.

Substances that encourage a light-sensitive rash (photo-dermatitis) and/or sunburn

Many substances are particularly effective at absorbing UV, and may therefore sensitize skin to UV so it burns or develops a rash in sunlight; later there may be increased pigmentation.

These can sensitize from within the body:

Foods

● Psoralens in celery, parsnips, parsley, figs, strawberries, buckwheat (which also inhibits melanin production) and Earl Grey tea (which contains bergamot oil).

Drugs

● Tetracyclines (tetracycline, doxycycline and demeclocycline).

● Phenytoin.

● Tretinoin.

● Phenothiazine.

● Certain non-steroidal anti-inflammatories (NSAIDs, such as ibuprofen), antidepressants, 'water tablets', blood-pressure drugs, anti-malarials, antihistamines, oral antidiabetic drugs, cancer drugs and oestrogen (e.g. in the Pill).

Herbal remedies

● St John's wort: problems are rare, but fair-skinned people may be particularly susceptible.

● Yarrow

Plants

● Marigold

● Cow parsley

● Giant hogweed

● Angelica

● Ground elder (goutweed/bishop's weed)

Those that can sensitize from outside the body include:

Aromatherapy oils

● Citrus oils (Bergapten, a psoralen in natural bergamot oil from the citrus bergamot tree – not the bergamot or 'bee balm' plant – is not present in synthetic bergamot oil.)

● Angelica root, verbena, rue and cumin oils, fig-leaf absolute, tagetes absolute and oil

Cosmetics and skin-care products

● Colourants such fluorescein and eosin in some nail polishes and lipsticks

● Alpha hydroxy acids (AHAs or fruit acids), because they thin the skin

● Hydantoin (in allantoin and urea)

Perfumes and aftershaves

● Plant oil psoralens called furocoumarins. The bergamot oil used in perfumes is synthetic (see citrus oils, above), which is good because natural oil is a potent light-sensitizer.

● Other plant oil psoralens – coumarins – which are less active than furocoumarins.

● Musk ambrette, a synthetic substance whose scent resembles that of musk, widely used as a perfume fixative and present in some aftershaves. However, it is only very occasionally found, because the International Fragrance Association (IFRA) recommends this should not be used for cosmetics, toiletries and other skin products.

Soaps and deodorants

● Plant oil psoralens called coumarins (see perfumes, above)

● A bactericide called trichlorocarbanilide

Sunscreens

● Plant oil psoralens called coumarins (see perfumes); 6-methylcoumarin was used in a popular sunscreen in the late 1970s, but the IFRA recommends it should not now be used as a fragrance in any product.

● p-aminobenzoic acid

part two Light and colour therapies

Many methods of using light and colour for healing have come down the centuries, and other ways have been added recently. Some of the therapies have historically been tinged with an air of hocus pocus, or associated with charlatans. But there's no need for this today, because there's now scientific evidence to back up many of them. Where there isn't yet enough evidence to prove or disprove a therapy's usefulness, I'll say so. Here you'll find brief explanations of each therapy, plus some practical tips, and a list of the conditions it may help.

You can use most of the therapies yourself. Some need special equipment, such as coloured gels (transparent acetate sheets), crystals, a light box, or a flashing mask (details of where to get many of these are in the Helplist, pages 156–7). Some call for things you'll already have around you, such as coloured clothing or food. But the most useful of all – sunlight exposure – needs no equipment... just the common sense to know when you've had enough!

Choosing a therapist

Some light and colour therapies, including medical PUVA treatment, precision-tinted lenses, and the use of lasers, require the aid of a doctor or other therapist. Before your treatment, check, if necessary, that the person belongs to a recognized professional body and is experienced with that particular therapy. And during the course of your treatment, evaluate your progress over the weeks so you can assess whether it really is helping.

Assessing health through a person's colour and brightness

An age-old way of assessing a person's health and wellbeing involves assessing their colour and brightness. For looking (and feeling) 'off-colour', or 'not too bright', is one of the first signs of many ailments. For example:

● Red face – over-exertion, anger, a fever, rosacea, blushing or menopausal hot flush

● Grey face – pain

● Grey-blue face – asthma, emphysema or arterial disease

● Blue face – coldness, poor circulation or a lack of oxygen

● Green face – nausea

● White face – anxiety or severe anaemia

● Red or purple rash – measles, blood disorder, vasculitis (inflamed blood vessels) or meningitis

● Yellow skin and eyes – jaundice

● Bloodshot eyes - hangover, overwork, crying, hay fever, air pollution or an eye infection or other disorder

● Dull eyes – depression or any illness

● Red tongue – vitamin B deficiency

● White tongue – fever

● Grey-blue nails – lung or heart disease

Sunlight

Sunlight is enjoyable and helps balance many hormones and neurotransmitters.

● Adjust exposure according to your skin type, age and any ailment; older people may need relatively more sunlight.

● If you can't go out, sit by a window; plain window glass transmits most light wavelengths well, though it cuts out some UV (especially UVB).

● Don't let yourself burn.

● Don't use sunscreen if you particularly need UV on your skin.

● If you wear glasses, spend some time outdoors each day without them, as lenses filter out some UV, and a little may be beneficial.

● Avoid too much sunlight if you have premature skin ageing, skin cancer, cold sores, cataracts, age-related macular degeneration, rosacea, lupus or light-sensitive migraine. Avoid sunlight if you are on light-sensitizing medication, or – for the recommended time – if you are having PUVA therapy.

Try for: acne, eczema, psoriasis, TB, high blood pressure, arterial disease, tooth decay, fibromyalgia, arthritis, osteoporosis, rickets, low sex drive, pre-menstrual syndrome, irregular periods, polycystic ovaries, fertility problems, anxiety, depression, Alzheimer's disease, shift-work disruption; jet-lag, pre-menstrual migraine, bulimia, Parkinson's disease, cancer (not skin), obesity, sleep problems, convalescence and multiple sclerosis.

Bright daylight filtered through cloud

This is less intense, provides less UV, and does not have such an even colour balance as direct sunlight.

● Light cloud reduces sunlight's UV by only 20–40 per cent, so take care not to burn when out on a dull day.

Try for: any condition that responds to sunlight.

Electric light

Certain ailments improve when electric lighting is brighter, better colour-balanced, or flicker-free. Certain types of electric lighting can help boost or rebalance various hormones and neurotransmitters, and help reset a disturbed body clock.

● Use a full-spectrum bulb or tube for a colour balance closer to that of sunlight. A 'daylight' bulb is very much second best to a full-spectrum one.

● See whether you feel better with something other than a cool-white fluorescent lighting.

● Use brighter light if necessary.

Try for (depending on the type of light): computer eyes, far sight, arterial disease, fibromyalgia, irregular periods, pre-menstrual syndrome, polycystic ovaries, low sex drive, irregular periods, fertility problems, anxiety, depression, jet-lag, pre-menstrual migraine, attention deficit disorder, Parkinson's disease, bulimia, obesity, cancer and convalescence.

Bright light from a light box or visor

This can help boost or rebalance various hormones and neurotransmitters, including serotonin, and reset a disturbed body clock.

Wearing a light visor – a baseball-style cap with battery-operated bright lights under its peak – lets you benefit from bright light while moving around.

Brighter light produces effects faster. Exposure for one hour a day is recommended from a light box producing 2,500 lux; 40 minutes from a 5,000-lux box; and 20 minutes from a 10,000-lux one. Some light boxes produce up to 10,000 lux of light. A visor's light may be adjustable to 3,000 lux; although it is near the eyes, tests prove it is safe.

● Use a box or visor (see pages 156-7), according to the product's instructions; most people find 20 to 40 minutes a day best. Anything over two hours a day may disturb your sleep.

● Check the model is UV-free.

Try for : cataracts, fibromyalgia, low sex drive, pre-menstrual syndrome, irregular periods, polycystic ovaries, fertility problems, anxiety, depression, Alzheimer's disease, shift-work disruption, jet lag, Parkinson's disease, bulimia, cancer, obesity and sleep problems, and during convalescence.

You'll see a light-box frame if you look around the outside of this spread; exposure to bright light from such a box can help prevent problems due to a lack of light.

UV light

Sunbeds and sun lamps produce intense UV from full-spectrum fluorescent tubes without diffusers. This can help boost the body's production of vitamin D and rebalance its levels of sex hormones, endorphins and serotonin. Modern sunbeds produce mainly UVA, but some UVB. They can encourage light-sensitive disorders and skin cancer if taken in excess. They can also make skin age faster. Remember that 'A' is for ageing!

- Avoid sunbeds if under 16 or red-haired. Also, if you have: fair skin that burns easily and tans slowly or not at all; lots of freckles or moles; or a history of skin cancer, or a close relative who has had it. Avoid it too if you take or use light-sensitizing substances (see pages 86–7), or have a light-sensitive condition. All these raise your skin cancer risk.
- The UK's Health and Safety Executive recommends no more than 20 sessions a year for people with none of these risk factors.
- Note that many dermatologists strongly disagree with using sunbeds at all.

The hand-held light-therapy device seen opposite produces polarized light plus some infra-red rays; together these can encourage the regeneration of healthy cells in inflamed or broken skin.

- Follow instructions about using the equipment and protecting your eyes.
- Remove cosmetics, deodorants and other skin products first.
- See a doctor if you have any skin changes that could indicate skin cancer (see page 55) as early treatment could be vital.
- UVA provides little protection against sunlight as it doesn't thicken skin like UVB, so protect your skin in sunlight afterwards as if you were still pale.

Try for (bearing in mind the above warnings): eczema, psoriasis, high blood pressure, arterial disease, tooth decay, fibromyalgia, arthritis, osteoporosis, rickets, low sex drive, pre-menstrual syndrome, irregular periods, polycystic ovaries, fertility problems, anxiety, depression and multiple sclerosis.

PUVA therapy

Medical PUVA therapy is a photodynamic therapy that involves taking a light-sensitive drug, then exposing skin to UVA. Do-it-yourself PUVA (little studied scientifically) involves eating light-sensitizing fruit or vegetables, then exposing skin to sunlight.

- Stay out of sunlight afterwards for the recommended time to avoid getting a light-sensitive rash.

- For a few days before and after PUVA, avoid foods containing natural light-sensitizing psoralens, such as celery, parsnips, parsley, figs, strawberries, buckwheat and Earl Grey tea, as they could cause a light-sensitive rash.

- For do-it-yourself PUVA, eat foods containing natural psoralens (see above) on a regular basis and get more sunlight on your skin.

- Avoid if you have any light-sensitizing or light-sensitive condition.

Try for: eczema, psoriasis and vitiligo.

Sunglasses

Sunglass lenses may contain chemicals that absorb light, be coated with a metallic layer that reflects light; or block half the light by absorbing only horizontally polarized light, which you get from glare. Large, close fitting, wrap-around sunglasses give the best protection.

- Some experts recommend wearing UV-blocking sunglasses whenever sunlight is bright enough to burn. Go without them at other times, because you need some bright light through your eyes for a healthy balance of hormones and neurotransmitters.

- Never look directly at bright sun.

Try for: cataracts, age-related macular degeneration, and bright-light sensitive migraine or epilepsy.

Polarized light

This contains 'coherent' light waves that travel in unison and can soothe inflammation, stimulate blood and lymph flow, and boost immunity. Laser light (see pages 106–107) is a type of polarized light.

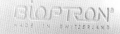

- Bioptron polarized-light devices, suitable for home use, produce light of 400–2000nm that is cool (so won't dry exposed tissue) and UV-free (so won't damage cells).

Try for: wounds, pressure sores, burns and leg ulcers; and possibly for acne, eczema, cold sores, psoriasis and warts.

Glasses (spectacles)

Spectacle lenses can change the direction of light rays to correct a refractive error. Over half the total US population wears glasses, and in the UK they are worn by 17 per cent of 5-15s, 35 per cent of 19-24s, 80 per cent of 45-54s and 96 per cent of over-55s, which is 53 per cent overall. Some people wear them for fear that not doing so would damage their eyesight. However, such damage is likely only in children with much poorer vision in one eye than the other, in which case not wearing glasses could suppress vision in the less well-sighted eye, possibly causing blindness that side ('amblyopia').

All lenses cut out some UV, the proportion depending on their material, thickness and surface; spectacle lenses can be coated with a UV-blocking layer to protect eyes further. Some research suggests that a little UV through the eyes boosts immunity and encourages retina cells to regenerate. This has led a few experts to suggest that glasses could encourage problems from UV deficiency, though only 'wrap-around' spectacles would prevent all unfiltered light from entering the eyes.

● However good your sight, having an eye test every two years helps detect eye conditions such as visual defects, glaucoma (raised eye-fluid pressure) and illnesses such as diabetes, which enables early treatment.

● Glasses may not be the only way of helping your eyesight or preventing deterioration; see the individual conditions in Part Three for suggestions.

● Take your glasses off outside for some time each day to let some full-spectrum light into your eyes.

● Although contentious, some experts believe that going without vision-correcting glasses for some time each day can help prevent vision worsening by encouraging ciliary muscle fitness.

Try for: poor night vision, short sight, long sight, far sight and astigmatism.

Contact lenses

The choice includes lenses that are soft, suitable for extended wear, disposable, coloured, and bifocal or multifocal (to help with both distant and near vision). The newest are hard lenses, worn only at night, which change the cornea's shape by putting pressure on different parts of it (see page 120).

● Clean reusable lenses scrupulously to avoid infection.

Try for: short sight, long sight, far sight and astigmatism.

Implanted lenses

These replace lenses dimmed by cataracts. During surgery a surgeon makes a 3mm (⅛in) cut, breaks up the lens with ultra-sound, sucks out the fragments, then implants the artificial lens.

● Sight usually recovers quickly.

● One in five people needs extra treatment with laser therapy within two years, but a new implanted-lens coating may reduce this figure.

Try for: cataracts.

Eye exercises

These include frequently looking away from close work and focusing on something far away; moving your forefinger from side to side, while moving your head to watch what's

behind the finger; and 'palming' – covering your eyes with the flats of your hands for a few seconds every half-hour.

● Remove glasses or contact lenses.

● For more information, contact the Bates Association (see page 156).

Try for: eyestrain, computer eyes, short sight, long sight, and far sight.

Pinhole glasses

These have black plastic 'lenses' studded with tiny holes. Wearing them immediately sharpens blurred vision. Research indicates that wearing them for a while each day permanently encourages better vision, possibly by exercising the ciliary muscles.

● Remove other glasses or contact lenses.

Try for: short sight, long sight and presbyopia.

Many people find that wearing these pinhole glasses makes poor sight clearer straight away – and some say that using them for a while each day gives permanently beneficial results.

Tinted lenses

One explanation for why particular tints help certain conditions is that they block wavelengths that irritate certain brain cells. Another is that coloured light fatigues over-excited brain cells, or rebalances levels of neurotransmitters and hormones.

● An 'intuitive colorimeter' with 140 choices can indicate whether any tint aids reading. Cerium Visual Technologies (see page 156) has a list of suitably equipped optometrists.

● An adult can try to discover which tint, if any, to use by fixing pieces of tinted overlay over their usual lenses, or plain lenses, for a week or more. Or they could try ready-made tinted glasses. However, a slight deviation from the required tint may make these useless.

● Anti-flicker (Freshlite – see page156) glasses help some flicker-sensitive disorders.

Try for: eyestrain, computer eyes, light-sensitive migraine or epilepsy, dyslexia and, perhaps, Parkinson's disease.

Clothing and decor colour

Just as we need each nutrient, so we need each wavelength of light. And just as we may need more or less of a nutrient when unwell, so may we need more or less of certain wavelengths when 'off colour'.

● Consider choosing wall-paint and soft-furnishing colours according to your personality. For example, reds, oranges and pinks may be good if you generally need or want stimulation; use blues and greens for a calming atmosphere.

● Choose clothing colours on the same basis, or according to current needs. Alternatively, use them to help project your image – red, for example, to project confidence, and blue, peacefulness.

Try for: anxiety, depression, obesity and sleep problems.

Brightly coloured food and drink

Looking at naturally coloured foods gives pleasure, which aids healing by decreasing stress hormones. Many plant pigments are antioxidant, and counteract damage caused by an excess of free radicals. The main green pigment is chlorophyll; red ones include lycopene; orange and yellow ones include beta-carotene and luteins; and purple ones include proanthocyanidins.

● Eat some red, orange, yellow, green and purple food each day.

Try for: eczema, psoriasis, ageing skin, cataracts, age-related macular degeneration, angina, heart attacks, transient ischaemic attacks, strokes, arthritis, depression and lupus.

Coloured light

Healing effects from the wavelengths we perceive as colours may be greater than from white light. In general, red stimulates and boosts healthy-cell renewal, while blue calms and reduces inflammation.

Coloured light is used by certain colour therapists, beauty therapists, cancer, eye and cosmetic surgeons, dermatologists and optometrists. Some shine coloured light on the whole body, others on the eyes or part of the skin; some use coloured flashing or laser light. Examples of coloured light therapies for

the eyes – or via the eyes – include tinted lenses, a mask that flashes red light, and coloured light directly shone into them (a therapy called syntonic optometry).

Some therapists shine it on chakras; colour acupuncturists shine a coloured light beam on to acupuncture points; colour reflexologists use it on 'reflex points' on the feet. Others recommend imagining coloured light (see pages 68–9). These therapies can be very relaxing but there is no evidence for specific healing effects.

● Use coloured bulbs; put a coloured gel (an acetate sheet from art-supply shops or theatre-lighting outlets) safely in front of an electric light; or put a coloured sleeve on a fluorescent tube (see Cocoon Light, page 156).

● Some therapists recommend always following a healing colour with its complementary colour (see page 42).

Try for: acne, eczema, psoriasis and cold sores (apply to the affected areas only); anaemia and high blood pressure (apply to the whole body).

'Solarized' liquids

Some colour therapists sometimes recommend drinking 'solarized' water – water put in a coloured glass container and stood in the sun for several hours. Water treated this way is certainly altered at a molecular level, and the therapists believe it can alter disturbed energy levels. While healing effects from drinking it have never been proven, it's easy to do and won't harm. It may even be worth a try!

● The container's colour should be strong, bright and clear.

● Use still mineral water.

● 'Solarize' for 3–4 hours in full sunlight.

● Flower and gem essences can be made this way.

● For anxiety or depression, choose a colour with immediate appeal. This may help you get in touch with underlying emotions: recognizing and naming them could help you manage your condition and move on when the time is right.

Consider for: eczema (red), psoriasis (red), cold sores (red), anaemia (red), high blood pressure (blue), and jaundice (blue or blue-green); for anxiety or depression, see the last tip (and see your doctor if necessary).

Colour acupuncture

This involves illuminating acupuncture points (acupoints) on the skin with coloured light, and is based on the proposition that energy (chi) flows along channels in the body called meridians. If this flow is considered blocked, overactive or weak, stimulation of associated acupoints is said to help. This stimulation can be done with fine needles (acupuncture), an electric current (electro-acupuncture), a magnet, heat (such as from burning herbs – moxibustion), fingertip pressure (acupressure), coloured light (colour acupuncture, chromopressure or colour-puncture), and perhaps even from a laser. Acupoints have lower electrical resistance than surrounding skin, and many correspond with myofascial trigger points in muscles, fascia or tendons (see Fibromyalgia, page 128). Some meridians correspond to pathways between the thin sheets of tough tissue ('fascia') that surround muscles and organs, and line the

Choosing Aura-Soma bottles, opposite, is a gentle, instinctive way of recognizing the symbolic importance to you of certain colours or colour combinations.

chest and abdomen. And it's been suggested that light energy can travel along meridians. Acupuncture itself provably helps heal some conditions (such as back pain and nausea). There is no proof that colour acupuncture works, but it could be worth trying.

Consider for: fibromyalgia and migraine.

Aura-Soma

This involves choosing coloured oils. Some bottles contain one colour, most two; a full set has 101 options. Many people feel intuitively drawn to some bottles, sensing a healing quality. Their colour, or colours, could symbolize an emotion or state the individual lacks, or one they wish to celebrate or recognize. For example, the blue 'Peace' bottle could symbolize the presence of calm (recognized or unrecognized), or the need for calm. The blue-over-violet 'Rescue' bottle could indicate a healing personality, or the need for healing. The yellow-over-gold 'Sunlight' bottle could suggest the presence of energy and joy, or a need for them. And the yellow-over-pink 'Rebirth' bottle, the fact that you have made a fresh start, or need one.

● Aura-Soma consultants say the first choice represents your soul, true aura or life purpose; the second, past problems you have overcome; the third, current wellbeing; the fourth, the future. There is some justification in allying the 'true self', past, present and future, with choices one to four, as self-image can be conceived in layers. A consultant can help you to a fuller understanding.

● Details from Aura-Soma's very 'new-age' website (see page 156).

Try for: anxiety, depression, bulimia, obesity and sleep problems.

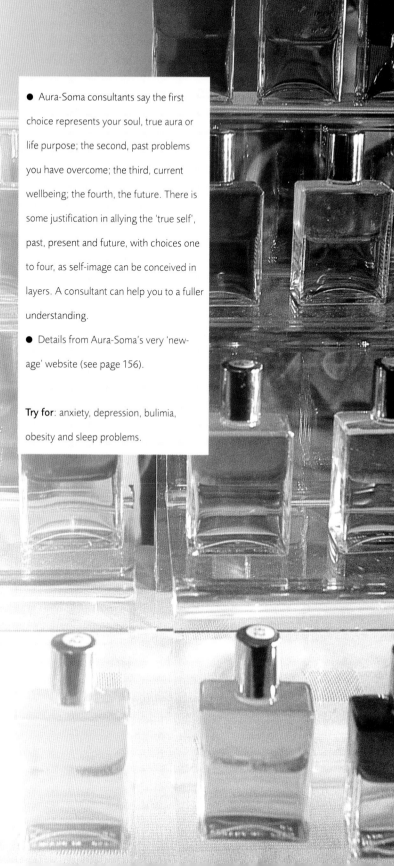

Flower therapy

Enjoying a flower's colour can inspire delight that stimulates immunity and boosts your levels of 'feel-good' endorphins. A colour can symbolize how you feel emotionally or spiritually, and magnify or counteract your state. Choosing an essence may help identify what you need or want.

Some people believe a flower's unique energy pattern can aid healing. They say this can be harnessed by 'solarizing' water to make a flower essence. There is considerable scientific evidence that water can have a 'memory', but no proof that this makes flower essences effective. Giving flowers of a particular colour can be a token of your feelings. And eating edible flowers provides antioxidant plant pigments.

- Choose colours you find inspiring, moving, calming or invigorating, depending on your needs. Particular colours may enhance certain feelings or states – such as orange for joy, red for passion and blue for contemplation; or make them easier to bear – perhaps orange for fatigue, red for depression, white for grief.
- Give red flowers for love, yellow for friendliness and mauve for sympathy, and use the colour to help you focus on a prayer or healing thought for them or for your relationship with the recipient.
- Edible flowers include nasturtiums, roses and borage.

Mystics see heaven in a grain of sand, and so beautiful are the light and colour of flowers and crystals that heaven shows there, too.

To prepare a flower essence:

Gather blossoms in the early morning, then leave them in a glass bowl of mineral water in the sun for three or four hours. Strain, and preserve the liquid 'essence' by adding a tablespoon of gin or vodka to three tablespoons of essence.

To take a flower essence, put two drops in some water and sip throughout the day.

Try for: anxiety, depression, bulimia, obesity and sleep problems.

Crystal healing

A 'crystal' is a chunk of crystallized mineral; gems or jewels are expensive, high-quality crystals. Feng-shui adherents believe that a crystal enhances a room's energy, while some people believe that placing a crystal on the body can alter the basic frequency ('vibration') of the body's energy. NASA astronauts are said to have carried quartz crystals charged with the frequency of the Earth's mechanical vibration to help protect their health.

Much crystal folklore is due to their enchanting colours and rainbows. Certainly, the symbolism of a crystal's colour could help by magnifying or calming your emotional or spiritual state.

Electrocrystal therapists charge a glass tube of crystals in salt water with an electro-magnetic field, and place it on a chakra for 30 minutes. They say this stimulates, calms or balances its energy, depending on what's needed. Crystal essences are made like flower essences, but using crushed crystals. Some colour therapists shine light through a crystal, saying this amplifies its energy. The evidence that such therapies work is largely anecdotal.

Crystal therapists say:

- Amethyst (purple silicon-dioxide quartz) may relax you.

- Rose quartz (pink silicon dioxide) may enhance contentment, and counteract poor self-esteem or feelings of being unloved.

- Lapis lazuli (blue sodium calcium aluminium sulphate silicate, with pyrite or calcite inclusions) may enhance perception and creativity, and counteract depression.

- Citrine (pale greenish-yellow silicon-dioxide quartz) may enhance optimism and counteract fear.

- Carnelian (reddish-brown silicon-dioxide quartz) may enhance compassion and energy, and counteract anger and apathy.

- Red crystals, such as rubies (red corundum or aluminium oxide) may stimulate you.

- Blue crystals such as sapphires (blue corundum) may calm you.

Aura reading

People who see an aura of light around the body say it can change in thickness, strength and colour according to the owner's emotional, spiritual or physical health. Differences in the aura on each side of the body are said to help locate a problem. Certainly the body does have an electro-magnetic field around it, and perhaps these people are able to see this even though most of us can't. Or perhaps, more prosaically, they are very good at reading body language. Aura readers are often healers who offer healing if necessary.

Fascinating though this is, there is no good scientific evidence yet that aura reading can reliably be used to detect or treat illness. So if you feel unwell, it's wise to get checked out by a doctor too.

Light as a water sterilizer

Sunlight can help disinfect drinking water, which is useful in parts of the world with a dirty water supply, little or no fuel for boiling, and little money for chemical sterilization.

Can some people really see an aura of light around the body... or is the aura opposite a product of their imagination, aided by clues picked up about a person's mood, energy and wellbeing?

Light as a blood cancer-cleanser or sterilizer

Researchers are investigating 'light transfusion'. For example, photomodification is a cancer treatment in which blood is taken from the body, treated with laser or other polarized light and then returned. Photo-phoresis ('extracorporeal photochemotherapy') involves giving someone a light-sensitizing agent, removing some blood, treating it with UVA and then returning it; this is used to treat a cancer called cutaneous T-cell lymphoma. UV irradiation of 5 per cent of the blood each day has been successfully used to treat infection with MRSA (methicillin-resistant *Staphylococcus aureus*). Its use for several other cancers, and for viral infections such as viral pneumonia and HIV (human immuno-deficiency virus) infection, is being investigated.

● To help reduce the population of micro-organisms in water, leave a plastic bottle of water in bright sunlight for several hours.

Visualization

Relaxing and creating mind pictures in light and colour can have a healing influence if these images are symbolically important or if the process induces biochemical changes. For the mind's power can alter the levels of various neurotransmitters, hormones and 'feel-good' endorphins, boost immunity and decrease pain.

● Do it for 10–20 minutes once or twice a day.

● If you have cancer, imagine cool fresh water washing your cancer cells away.

● If stressed, imagine overcoming the problem, or doing something relaxing.

● Use the visualization techniques on pages, 68–9.

● Incorporate visualization into prayer, imagining, for example, that you can see God, and that God is healing you.

Try for: eczema, psoriasis, rosacea, wounds, bedsores and ulcers, TB, high blood pressure, angina, heart attacks and strokes, anxiety, depression, migraine, bulimia, cancer, obesity, convalesence and sleep problems.

Neurolinguistic programming (NLP)

This re-educates the memory and imagination so that they no longer follow established pathways that harm wellbeing. An important feature is to practise visualizing new sets of images that make you feel better.

● Think of a past experience that distresses you, then imagine it happening differently, in a positive, non-destructive way. This will help you to handle similar experiences differently in the future.

● Think of what triggers any harmful habit, and imagine doing something constructive instead.

Try for: any illness encouraged by habits such as an unhealthy diet, lack of exercise or the inability to manage stress effectively.

Photodynamic therapy

'Drug-light' therapy involves having a light-sensitive acid or other substance applied to your skin, or taking or being injected with a light-sensitive substance. Cancer cells absorb more of these agents than normal cells, and fluoresce when irradiated with UV, which may help identify their position. Some days later, light (usually red, and sometimes laser) is shone onto abnormal skin, or into the body via a fibreoptic endoscope. The light-sensitive substance absorbs photons of this light. This energizes its molecules, making them 'excited' or unstable. They can then pass this energy to oxygen, creating unstable oxygen particles (free radicals) that will hopefully destroy the cancer cells by oxidizing them.

PUVA is a type of photodynamic therapy.

● Avoid bright light on the skin for up to six weeks, depending on the agent used.

Try for: cold sores, psoriasis, warts, certain cancers and macular degeneration.

Screening

Certain lights make some tissue glow, which can be useful for screening certain conditions.

For lung cancer, researchers thread a tube into an airway and illuminate it with blue laser light. This makes normal cells look green and cancer cells red, and highlights very early cancer, enabling more successful treatment.

For hard-to-see nits (headlice eggs), researchers are developing a shampoo that makes them glow in UV.

For fungal scalp infection, UV makes infected hairs fluoresce with greenish-blue light.

Try for fungal scalp infection and (if available) lung cancer and nits .

Flashing or 'pulsed' white or coloured light

Therapeutic devices that flash light in the eyes at up to 50 pulses a second can boost endorphins and balance certain neurotransmitters. This can reduce pain, encourage relaxation and treat several ailments. It may also help if a stressful event has led to vision being lost in one eye, or has constricted a visual field. In some people the brain is particularly sensitive to certain wavelengths in flashing light, or to sudden flashes of bright white light. An alert

There's good evidence that wearing a mask that flashes light safely into the eyes, opposite, can have a profound influence on certain bodily functions, and can help right the pre-menstrual syndrome.

person can see light flickering at 40 flashes a second, a sleepy one at 30 flashes a second.

Exposure of skin to bright pulsed white light can treat freckles, blotchy discoloration, birthmarks, thread veins and tattoos, remove hair, and reduce scars and fine lines by creating heat that breaks down dilated blood vessels or patches of pigment. Pulses of laser light are particularly intense.

For eyes:

● 30 flashes a second is most popular.

● If using a flashing light mask, see whether changing the flash rate helps.

● Use a flashing light mask under medical supervision first if you have flicker-senstive seizures or are susceptible to migraines (though a device that shines light alternately into each eye is extremely unlikely to provoke an attack).

Try for: computer eyes, pre-menstrual syndrome, anxiety, migraine, seizures, obesity.

For skin:

● If three to five treatments don't work, don't bother with more.

Try for: prematurely ageing skin, rosacea.

Bionic eye

Researchers are working on the bionic eye, a high-tech electronic gadget which gives sight to the blind. A tiny camera on spectacles converts light into electronic messages which are radioed to a microchip inserted behind the retina or by the optic nerve, and then relayed to the visual cortex. This currently enables vague shapes to be seen, but refinements should produce better 'sight' in future. Sadly, a bionic eye will help only those who once had sight.

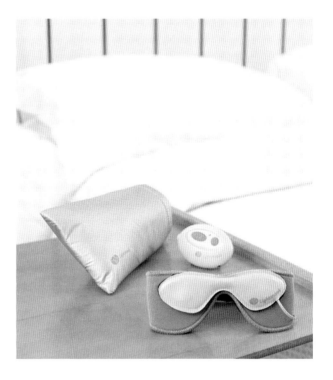

Laser therapy

Laser light is a very intense, highly focused, pulsed beam of single-wavelength (monochromatic, or one colour), polarized (or 'coherent') light that comes from irradiated gas, coloured liquid, or crystals. Its colour is chosen to match the light-absorbency of the structures being treated.

At its most powerful, laser light can hit the moon. Used on the body, it can heat tissue, which means that surgeons can use it as a scalpel to cut away unwanted or diseased tissue. An ophthalmic surgeon may use it, for example, to stick down a detached retina, or to treat glaucoma (increased pressure of the fluid in the front of the eye, between the lens and cornea). It can also be used to stop tiny blood vessels bleeding. Less powerful laser light is used for photodynamic therapy (see page 104) and plastic surgery. And researchers are investigating a cancer treatment called blood photomodification (see page 102).

Cosmetic surgeons can make skin look younger by using a laser to destroy the skin's superficial layer: as it heals, lines, wrinkles and blotches are greatly reduced. However, the

It would be better for the person who did the painting opposite to work out their own interpretation of the emotions behind it – but discussing it with someone else could give them valuable clues.

● If considering a cosmetic laser treatment, discuss it with two or three different clinics so that you know you will be treated with the most appropriate laser. Some are more effective for certain operations, or have fewer side effects than others, but not every clinic has the best one for every procedure. For example, for skin rejuvenation the erbium:YAG (YAG standing for yttrium aluminium garnet) laser is much better than the CO_2 laser – which may cause permanently white patches of skin, and make skin heal slowly.

● If using a laser pointer when showing slides to an audience, avoid pointing it at anyone's eyes; a very brief exposure to the soft laser light from such a pointer, however, is very unlikely to do any permanent damage.

Try for: rosacea, short sight, long sight, astigmatism, age-related macular degeneration, snoring, heavy periods, endometriosis and cancer.

effects may last only for a year or so, and a very few people end up with unacceptable scarring or pigmentation. Cosmetic surgeons can also use a laser to treat thread veins, birthmarks and ugly scars, and to remove tattoos by making their pigments disintegrate (though red pigments are hard to destroy). They train other therapists to use laser light to destroy unwanted hair.

Art therapy

This encourages the expression of conscious and unconscious emotions, which aids their recognition so that you can find ways of dealing with them; it also releases them in a non-damaging way. Art therapy can help heal depression, 'stress', and unconsciously motivated behaviours which protect against painful feelings. These behaviours include addictions (such as overeating, drinking too much, or being a workaholic or shopaholic) and antisocial actions (such as bullying and constantly putting people down).

Art therapy involves making pictures with paints, crayons, pastel sticks, charcoal or coloured pencils, or making models or other creations. Give yourself the freedom to do what comes naturally, so your use of shapes, colours, lightness and darkness will symbolize the way you are feeling.

● Afterwards, try to work out, if you don't already know, which emotions your artwork symbolizes.

● Consider working with a qualified art therapist if you feel very upset or depressed.

Try for: anxiety, depression, obesity and bulimia.

part three Light-responsive conditions

All these ailments respond to light, and for some it's the most valuable means of prevention and treatment. Whatever your ailment, aim to identify the trigger, if possible, as avoidance is often the best solution.

Tell your doctor if you are on medication, and are using light therapy or taking herbal remedies or plant hormones, as some of these may react with certain drugs.

If you suspect food sensitivity, eliminate suspects one at a time for three weeks each to identify the culprit. Meanwhile, ask a doctor or dietitian for advice, if necessary, on maintaining a healthy diet, and always do this for a child.

Some of the tips suggest eating more foods rich in particular nutrients. This list shows which they are:

Beta-carotene orange, red and dark-green fruit and vegetables.

Vitamin B meat, fish, dairy, eggs, beans, peas, green leafy vegetables, mushrooms, nuts, seeds, wholegrains.

Vitamin B6 beans, peas, green leafy vegetables, mushrooms, nuts, seeds, wholegrains.

Folic acid dairy, eggs, nuts, fruit, vegetables (especially green leafy), beans, peas, wholegrains.

Vitamin C fruit (especially citrus, kiwis, strawberries), vegetables.

Vitamin D oily fish, egg yolk, full-fat dairy, nuts, cold-pressed vegetable oils, vitamin D-fortified food such as breakfast cereals and margarines.

Vitamin E meat, fish, dairy, eggs, green leafy vegetables, beans, peas, sweet potatoes, mangoes, nuts, seeds, wholegrains.

Vitamin K liver, eggs, green leafy vegetables, cauliflower, turnips, beans, wholegrains.

Calcium tinned fish eaten with their bones, shellfish, dairy, eggs, beans, peas, lentils, nuts, seeds, wholegrains.

Chromium shellfish, dairy, wholegrains.

Copper liver, seafood, cheese, egg yolk, green vegetables, apricots, cherries, figs.

Iron meat, shellfish, eggs, green leafy vegetables, mushrooms, beans, peas, nuts, seeds, wholegrains.

Magnesium meat, fish, eggs, green leafy vegetables, mushrooms, beans, peas, nuts, seeds, wholegrains.

Potassium fruit, vegetables.

Selenium meat, fish, dairy, eggs, green leafy vegetables, mushrooms, garlic, beans, peas, wholegrains.

Zinc meat, dairy, fish, shellfish, root vegetables, beans, peas, garlic, nuts, seeds, wholegrains.

Omega-6 fatty acids avocados, beans, corn, seeds, seed oils.

Omega-3 fatty acids green-leafy vegetables, broccoli, beans, walnuts and their oil, pumpkin seeds and their oil, linseeds, wholegrains, rapeseed (canola) oil, oily fish (such as sardines, herrings, salmon).

Plant pigments flavonoids in brightly coloured fruits and vegetables, including proanthocyanidins in blue, black and dark-red berries; lutein and zeaxanthin in eggs, corn, red grapes, pumpkin, orange peppers.

Quercetin onions, tea.

Plant hormones bean sprouts, fennel, celery, parsley, beans, peas, lentils, chick peas, wholegrains, seeds, potatoes, carrots, beetroot, cabbage, cherries, plums, rhubarb, olives.

Salicylates fruit (especially the peel), vegetables, seeds, nuts.

Fibre fruits, vegetables, wholegrains.

Low-glycaemic-index foods proteins, fats, nuts, vegetables (not root vegetables), fruit (not bananas, grapes, pineapple or water melon).

High-glycaemic-index foods root vegetables, bread, most breakfast cereals, white rice.

Skin

Acne

Causes include over-sensitivity of the sebaceous glands to testosterone, blockage of follicles by sticky dead cells, overgrowth of *Propionibacterium acnes* bacteria, and sebum changes. Triggers include a falling pre-menstrual oestrogen level, the progestogen-only Pill, the polycystic ovary syndrome, heat, humidity, stress and certain medications.

How light and colour can help

1. Expose skin to bright daylight for at least 15 minutes a day, as this makes skin oils more antiseptic.
2. Consider bathing in red and blue light from a Dermalux light box for 15 minutes a day for 12 weeks; blue light may kill bacteria and red will reduce inflammation and aid healing.
3. Try polarized light therapy.

Other tips

● Exercise daily.
● Wash with a soapless cleansing bar or face-wash lotion or gel.
● Choose oil-free cosmetic products.
● Splash skin daily with a pint of water containing a tablespoon of vinegar and two drops each of petitgrain, juniper berry and geranium oils.
● Treat blackheads with salicylic acid cream, gel or wash, and consider using a blackhead extractor or strips.
● Treat mild acne with benzoyl peroxide cream or gel, or tea tree oil.

● Puncture a yellow-headed spot with a sterilized needle, squeeze gently, then dab with tea tree oil.
● Try a multivitamin and mineral supplement.
● Try two teaspoons a day of sarsaparilla (wild liquorice) tincture for a month.

Doctors may also recommend *for blackheads*: retinoid gel, lotion or cream (not in pregnancy; avoid sunlight and UV afterwards) or azelaic acid cream. *For mild acne*: antibiotic solution, lotion or gel, perhaps alternated with a retinoid product; or vitamin B3 cream. *For moderate acne*, if the above doesn't work: oral antibiotics (if on the Pill, use additional contraception for a month), or a cyproterone acetate Pill. *For severe acne,* if two courses of antibiotics don't work: oral isotretinoin.

Prematurely ageing skin, and skin cancer

Too much sunlight, especially if combined with smoking and a poor diet, encourages premature ageing of the skin and skin cancer (see page 55).

How light and colour can help

1. See pages 56–8 for protective measures.
2. Coloured-light therapy can reduce lines, freckles and thread veins. For example, red light (660nm) makes cells called macrophages in the skin produce growth factors that stimulate fibroblasts to make more collagen and elastin.
3. For age spots, consider pulsed light treatment; laser light can help but is harsher.

4. Consider photodynamic therapy (see page 104); this may use blue light for age spots, and red light for rodent ulcers or Bowen's disease (see page 55).

5. Eat more foods rich in plant pigments.

6. Applying bacterial-DNA repair enzymes to the skin of people with xeroderma pigmentosum – a rare condition with a very high rate of skin cancer due to the defective repair of sun-induced DNA mutations – greatly reduces the cancer risk. Products containing these enzymes may one day become generally available.

Other tips

● Eat more foods rich in omega-3s (to reduce burning) and antioxidants (beta-carotene, vitamins C and E, selenium and zinc).

● Apply cream containing alpha-hydroxy (fruit) acids, but protect skin from sunlight afterwards.

● See a doctor if an age spot or mole darkens, becomes patchy, enlarges, itches, reddens, develops an irregular border, bleeds or ulcerates, in case it's becoming cancerous.

Doctors may also recommend *for age spots*: 5 per cent 5-fluorouracil or 0.05 per cent tretinoin cream, or cell-killing cream. *For seborrhoeic keratoses*: removal. *For solar keratoses*: observation (as there's a small cancer risk), or treatment with diclofenal gel (a non-steroidal, anti-inflammatory product), freezing, a laser, scraping, cautery or cell-killing cream. *For rodent ulcers*: applying imiquimod cream daily for six weeks; then, if not successful, scraping, freezing or

irradiation. Imiquimod is a comparatively new treatment and not all doctors try it first, though it has the advantage of not increasing scarring. *For malignant melanomas*: surgery and, perhaps, chemotherapy and radiotherapy; photodynamic therapy, immunity-boosting interferon and vaccines are under investigation.

Eczema

Triggers include house-dust-mite droppings, skin cells and mites in pet fur, and certain foods, infections, moulds, drugs and chemicals (in detergent, perfume and sunscreen). Heat, dry air, smoke, stress, sand, chlorine and rough clothing worsen itching.

How light and colour can help

1. Get more bright light on skin outdoors.

2. Eat more celery, citrus fruit, figs, parsley, parsnips and watercress; their psoralens may boost sunlight's healing.

3. Eat more foods rich in plant pigments.

4. Consider polarized light or, for severe eczema, UVB or PUVA.

5. Broken skin may heal better with red light (660nm) treatment.

Other tips

● Soak for 20 minutes daily in water containing either bath oil, two cups of powdered oatmeal (for itching), a handful of salt dissolved in hot water (not for broken skin), or a pint of chamomile tea.

● Wash with a soapless cleansing bar or, for bad eczema, emulsifying ointment.

● Moisturize well.

● Try Seven Herb Cream (from Bioforce, see page 156), hemp-seed oil cream, or hemp-seed oil from a capsule.
● Cover open skin.
● Soothe with a compress soaked in cold borage, chickweed, chamomile, marigold or carrot tea.
● Eat more foods rich in vitamins B, C and E, zinc and selenium.
● Take borage or evening-primrose oil capsules, for gamma-linoleic acid.

Doctors may also recommend steroid cream.

Cold sores

These occur when *Herpes simplex* viruses resting in a nerve are activated. Sores appear in skin supplied by that nerve. Possible triggers include sunshine, stress, infection, menstruation, fatigue and skin damage.

How light and colour can help

1. Think whether you were in the sun a lot before your sore appeared. If so, keep out of the sun until it's better and protect lips in future with a lip balm containing sun block, especially when you are feeling unwell. Don't let other people use the balm.
2. Encourage healing with red light (660nm).
3. Ask a dermatologist about photodynamic therapy. This involves either applying light-sensitive dye (chrome yellow is especially effective), and then exposing the sore to blue-violet light (450nm) for 30 minutes four times over two days; or applying some other photosensitive drug and using white fluorescent light.

Other tips

● See whether keeping it moist or dry helps most. To moisten, apply any ointment, cream or oil with a cotton bud; for added healing, choose St John's wort oil (red 'heart of Jesus' oil), lavender or tea tree oil, melissa ointment (from Herpes Viruses Association, see page 157), or vitamin A or E oil from a capsule. To dry, use surgical spirit, witch hazel or an over-the-counter remedy containing iodine, menthol, ammonia, phenol or alcohol. Some people find applying black coffee helps.
● Eat two raw garlic cloves a day.
● Have more lysine-rich food (beans, lentils, cabbage, potatoes, buckwheat, rye) and less arginine-rich food (nuts, seeds, chocolate, wheat), as altering the dietary balance of these two amino acids can make cold sores less likely. You could also try a daily lysine supplement.
● Eat more foods rich in vitamin C, flavonoids and zinc, and consider taking these nutrients as a supplement.
● Try not to touch the sore; if you do, wash hands well and dry on kitchen paper.
● Don't kiss anyone, especially if they are very young, unwell, pregnant, or have eczema.
● Don't perform oral sex on your partner, even through a condom; cold sore herpes viruses occasionally cause genital infection, and vice versa, and viruses have been known to pass through microscopic holes in the latex rubber of a condom.

Doctors may also recommend cream or tablets of an antiviral drug such as aciclovir.

Psoriasis

This produces silvery, flaky patches on the knees, elbows and/or scalp, perhaps with pitted nails, and arthritis. The flaking results from an abnormally rapid turnover of skin cells. Psoriasis is an autoimmune (self-allergic) condition, meaning immune cells turn against the skin instead of being protective, and it often runs in families. Possible triggers include sunburn, stress, smoking, cold weather, injury, hormone changes, respiratory infection, certain medications, alcohol and sensitivity to gluten (in wheat, barley, rye and, perhaps, oats).

How light and colour can help

1. Expose patches to sunlight each day, if possible; 15 minutes may be enough in strong sunlight. Applying paraffin jelly or other oily lubricant increases the benefit as long as it doesn't contain sunscreen! This helps three people in four.
2. Bathe in electric light or sunlight filtered through a red acetate-gel sheet for 30 minutes a day. If using electric light, don't let the gel get too hot.
3. Bathe in UVB light – but discuss this with a dermatologist first.
4. Discuss the possibility of PUVA treatment with a dermatologist. For mild, do-it-yourself PUVA: eat some celery, liquidized whole citrus fruit, figs, parsley, parsnips or watercress (which contain small amounts of psoralens), and bathe in sunlight (or just daylight) every day. A dermatologist may suggest another sort of photodynamic therapy – painting patches with a light-sensitive acid

and then bathing them in red light for 2–4 hours. Photodynamic therapy may help associated arthritis too, possibly by reducing the number of activated T cells (a type of immune cell) in the skin, and therefore reducing the autoimmune response.
5. Exposure to polarized light is said to help.
6. If your psoriasis is stress-related, use visualization to aid relaxation.
7. Try spicing food with turmeric.

Other tips

● If possible, identify, then avoid or minimize any triggers.
● Soothe with cream containing anti-inflammatory plants, such as *Mahonia aquifolia* (oregon grape), marigold (calendula), oak, or *Melia azadirachta* (neem); aloe gel; or a moist banana skin.
● Eat more foods rich in folic acid, selenium, zinc and omega-3 fatty acids; consider taking a supplement of cod liver oil or fish oil for a month to see if it helps.
● Try cutting down on meat and dairy produce for a month.
● Eat a gluten-free diet (one with no wheat, barley, rye and oats) for a month; consult a dietitian or doctor if unsure what to eat, or if altering a child's diet.

Doctors may also recommend creams (for dryness), salicylic acid or dithranol products (for flaking), and tar (for inflammation). Other possibilities are calcipotriol (a vitamin D-like drug), steroid or retinoid (a vitamin A-like drug) skin products, and oral anti-fungal or cytotoxic (cell-killing) drugs.

Warts

These are caused by a viral infection, usually with human papillomaviruses. When on the feet they are called verrucas. Warts usually spread by direct contact with an infected person, whereas verrucas are most often picked up in warm, moist conditions, such as bathrooms or changing rooms, after someone with verrucas has walked there with bare feet. The average wart disappears in nine months and many people never get another. But some warts last for years.

How light and colour can help

1. Photodynamic – 'drug-light' – therapy is more than three times as successful as freezing for resistant warts. For this, dermatologists paint them with a photosensitive drug (such as aminolaevulinic acid), then expose them to white or red light.
2. Polarized light therapy may be worth trying.

Other tips

● Freeze off a wart at home, using an aerosol (see Wartner aerosol, page 157) that releases a deep-freezing combination of gases.
● If you have a verruca, don't walk barefoot in bathrooms or changing rooms used by other people, or around swimming pools, unless you wear a waterproof foot cover.
● Apply a paint, gel, paste or plaster containing a caustic substance such as salicylic acid or podophyllin; tea tree oil; clear nail polish; the white sap from dandelion stalks; the orange sap from *Chelidonium majus* (greater celandine or wartgrass) stalks; apple cider vinegar; or a sliver of garlic. Then cover with a sticking plaster. Repeat every day, or as directed on the product's packaging.
● Boost immunity with plenty of foods rich in beta carotene and vitamins C and E, regular light-to-moderate exercise, and effective stress-managment.

Doctors or chiropodists may also recommend a more concentrated caustic preparation; or they may offer scraping, paring or freezing.

Skin wounds, pressure sores, burns and leg ulcers

Get expert help to close and dress open skin, and to advise on treatment, unless the area is very small.

How light and colour can help

1. A few minutes' daily exposure to polarized light (such as that provided by a Bioptron light-therapy device, see page 156) can aid healing, partly by boosting the blood supply.
2. Visualize white cells engulfing infecting organisms.

Other tips

● Keep active.
● Raise your leg when sitting, if you have a leg ulcer.
● Don't smoke.
● Cover with a plaster, film, or other non-adherent dressing to keep it moist (not soggy), as moist skin cells multiply twice as fast as dry ones. Choose a 'breathable' covering to help superficial cuts heal faster, and a non-adherent dressing for burns.

● Boost your circulation by exercising daily and keeping warm.

● Change the dressing only every two days, if possible.

● Nourish the skin with a healthy diet.

● Consider supplements of vitamins A, C and E, selenium, zinc, and fish oil.

Doctors may also recommend tetanus vaccination, antibiotics, and stitches or other surgery. Infected leg ulcers can be treated with maggots to clear dead tissue and pus; low-dose ultrasound may help too.

Rosacea

One in 10 women aged 30-55 has intense bouts of blushing. If continued over the years, rosacea can enlarge small veins, and make skin swollen, permanently red and, perhaps, painful, with a pimply rash and inflamed eyes and eyelids. At worst, the nose becomes thick and red.

Possible causes include a mite infestation of the hair follicles, a digestive disorder associated with a lack of stomach acid, and over-sensitivity of small blood vessels. Rosacea can run in families, is commoner in fair-skinned women, and may be associated with migraine. Possible triggers include sunlight, extremes of weather, stress, coffee, tea, cocoa, alcohol (especially red wine) and certain foods – anything spiced, fermented, soured, pickled, marinated or smoked, as well as liver, steak, yoghurt, cheese (not cottage), aubergines, avocados, spinach, citrus fruit, tomatoes, bananas, red plums, raisins, figs, chocolate, vanilla, soy sauce, yeast extract, dark vinegar, coffee, cocoa and tea.

How light and colour can help

1. Avoid strong sunlight if you find this makes it worse.

2. Use a factor-15 (or higher) sunscreen containing minerals (titanium dioxide or zinc oxide, which reflect light) rather than chemical filters which could irritate the skin.

3. Mask the redness with green-toned foundation or camouflage make up.

4. Consider laser or pulsed-light treatment for unsightly broken veins.

5. Use visualization to aid relaxation.

Other tips

● Identify, then avoid or minimize any triggers, if possible.

● Avoid using products containing fragrances, oils and alcohols (found in many toners, and hair sprays and gels).

● Eat more foods rich in vitamin B (to nourish nerves in blood-vessels, vitamin C and flavonoids (to strengthen blood-vessels, and, if you have hot flushes, plant hormones (to balance hormones).

● Take supplements of vitamin B, vitamin C with flavonoids, betaine hydrochloride (to supplement stomach acid) and isoflavones (plant hormones); try each separately for a month to see if they help.

● Try gentle massage.

Doctors may also recommend metronidazole gel, long-term oral antibiotics (tetracycline), or cream containing isotretinoin (a vitamin A derivative).

Melasma

Also called the 'mask of pregnancy', this brown pigmentation is caused by an excess of melanin in certain areas of light-exposed skin, most often on the face and neck. It tends to appear in the summer, and generally fades during the winter. The trigger is exposure to sunlight in combination either with a raised level of hormones (from pregnancy or the Pill), or the presence of a light-sensitizing substance (see pages 86–7) on the skin.

How light and colour can help

1. Use a high-factor sunscreen on light-exposed skin to prevent further pigmentation.
2. Take care not to put any known light-sensitizing substances – such as some perfumes – on your skin, or to touch your face after handling such a substance with your fingers.
3. Laser therapy can lighten melasma which doesn't respond to other treatments. A pulsed dye laser is best for melasma in which the melanin is relatively superficial (in the epidermis); a Q-switched laser is more effective when the melanin is deeper (in the dermis). A doctor can distinguish between superficial and deep pigmentation by shining UV light from a Wood's lamp on to the skin. This makes superficial pigmentation look darker, and deeper pigmentation look lighter or even the same colour as normal skin.

Other tips

● Conceal the marks with extra make-up, or use special 'camouflage' make-up made for hiding birthmarks.

● Avoid lightening brown patches with over-the-counter bleaching creams containing hydroquinone or mercury. These are now banned in many countries because although they can bleach the skin, they can also cause permanent blotchiness, not just locally, but elsewhere on the body too. Even worse, prolonged use can lead to kidney damage.

Doctors may also recommend *for melasma that doesn't respond to the above tips,* a combination of three creams: tretinoin, betamethasone (a steroid) and a gentle derivative of hydroquinone.

Vitiligo

This is a common disorder in which pale patches appear on the skin, usually symmetrically on both sides of the body, and most often on the face, hands, feet, armpits or groin. It usually begins in the person's 20s or 30s. The patches contain no melanin, which means sunlight's UV doesn't tan this skin, but can make it burn. Even worse, it can make the patches spread. Premature greying of hair occurs in one in three affected people.

Vitiligo can run in families and follow an injury. It is often an autoimmune disorder, mean ing the body's antibodies attack melanin producing cells, and is sometimes associated with another autoimmune disorder, such as insulin-dependent diabetes, pernicious anaemia, and a type of thyroid gland inflammation called Hashimoto's thyroiditis. It can also result from sunburn, stress, injury, steroid injections and certain chemicals on the skin. Sometimes vitiligo is mimicked by a fungal skin infection that causes patches of depigmented and, perhaps, flaky skin. This is a type of ringworm known as tinea (or pityriasis) versicolor. It's due to an overgrowth of normal skin fungi called *Malassezia* (or *Pityrosporum*) *furfur*, and is treated with anti-fungal cream; twice-weekly applications of selenium sulphide shampoo (Selsun) for three months work well too.

How light and colour can help

1. Protect pale patches with sunblock.
2. PUVA treatment is the most successful therapy; consider asking your doctor about it, or try a do-it-yourself version. Medical PUVA leads to some repigmentation in 60–80 per cent of people, and a cosmetically successful result in up to 20 per cent. But this is slow to happen, and may need over 100 treatments.
3. Conceal patches with camouflage make-up.

Other tips

● Avoid occupational exposure to rubber, or phenol derivatives.

Doctors may also recommend daily supplements or fortnightly injections of folic acid and of vitamins B12 and C; lightening skin around vitiligo patches on the face with a bleaching cream.

Polymorphic light eruption

This very itchy rash consists of small blisters on light-exposed skin, perhaps with general reddening and swelling. It may be due to over-exposure to UVA light caused by the use of a UVB sunscreen that lets UVA through.

The lack of any warning sunburn means you can get too much UVA without realizing. Irritation in the presence of sunlight by a sunscreen, cosmetic, skin-care product or perfume on the skin is another possibility, though uncommon. Healed skin may have extra pigmentation.

How light and colour can help

1. Keep out of the light, and keep all products off the skin until the rash heals.
2. Use a combined UVA and UVB sunscreen, or simply shade or cover your skin in sunlight.
3. If you still get the rash, stop using any other products on the affected skin before going out in the sun, and reintroduce them one at a time, leaving a week between each one.

Other tips

● Soothe skin with a cold compress such as a flannel soaked in ice-cold water.
● Relieve itching by bathing in tepid water containing two cups of fine oatmeal, or 500ml (1 pint) chamomile tea.
● Eat more omega-3 fatty acids to help reduce inflammation.

Doctors may also recommend steroid cream and preventive UV therapy before the summer, or a sunny holiday.

Eyes

Eyestrain

Too much close work can make eyes ache.
One reason is the continued and unrelieved
contraction of the ciliary muscles, which make
the lenses in your eyes 'fatter' when focusing
on something close to for a long time without
a break. This may interfere with the flow of
fluid in the front part of the eye, making the
eyes feel 'full', which may make you want to
press and rub your closed eyes to relieve the
feeling. When you look away, your distant
vision may temporarily be worse than usual
because eyestrain has fatigued your ciliary
muscles. Close work continued for many
months encourages permanent short sight.
Headaches can indicate an eyesight problem,
'computer eyes' (see below), or stress.

How light and colour can help

1. Glance a long way away every few minutes
to change your eyes' focus and relax your
hard-working ciliary muscles.
2. Have a 5–10 minute break every hour, and
don't do other close work instead!
3. Have an eye test in case you need glasses.
4. There's fairly strong evidence that eyestrain
from reading can be lessened in some people
by wearing glasses with individually chosen,
precision-tinted lenses.

Other tips

● Try more effective stress-management
techniques, if necessary.
● See your doctor if headaches continue.

'Computer eyes'

A VDU screen can cause eyestrain (see above)
and dry the surface of the eyes, making them
feel uncomfortable. Glare from the screen due
to window or lighting reflections can be
uncomfortable and encourage headaches. Both
headaches and migraine can also result from a
screen's inherent flicker, as this is perceived by
the brain even though it is invisible to the eye.
The changing extra-low-frequency electromagnetic field (emf) associated with a
switched-on computer creates small electric
currents in the body. Some experts think these
can cause headaches, depression, anxiety,
fatigue and poor concentration, memory and
sleep in those who are 'electrically sensitive'.
The UK's National Radiation Protection Board
says there is no conclusive evidence, but has
called for further research.

There is a large static emf between you and
the screen, because the screen has a large
positive voltage and your body is earthed. So
your face automatically attracts positively
charged airborne dust. This can cause rashes
and make your eyes feel gritty. This emf also
reorientates retinal nerve cells, which can
reduce visual clarity and the ability to judge an
object's position. Finally, at least one researcher
believes that the emfs from VDUs can make
eyes bloodshot and at worst even damage the
cornea, causing shallow ulcers called erosions.

How light and colour can help

1. Reduce the screen's brightness.
2. Position your screen to avoid reflections
from windows or lights.
3. Buy a mesh screen to reduce dazzle.

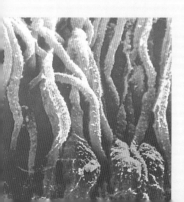

4. Cover your eyes with your hands for a few seconds every half-hour. The light level changes from this 'palming' may make you more comfortable.

5. If sensitive to screen flicker, avoid fluorescent lighting as this produces additional flicker, especially if it is relatively 'cold' or blue in tone.

6. If sensitivity to screen flicker causes headaches or eyestrain, consider using Freshlite sunglasses which have tinted lenses that eliminate flicker (see page 156).

7. Consider using a laptop with a liquid crystal display (LCD) screen, as this produces a much smaller emf and is flicker-free.

Other tips

● Take a break for 5–10 minutes every hour to give your eyes a rest.

● Splash your face with cold water every hour or so to remove dust.

● Blink frequently, to wash away dust and moisten your eyes.

● Consider buying an antenna (Tecno AO, page 157) to put on your VDU. This emits a magnetic oscillator signal, said to counteract harmful effects of the VDU's emf by encouraging an alpha-wave rhythm in the brain. The evidence is hopeful, if scanty.

Poor night vision

'Low-luminance' or night myopia is short sight in dim light (when you don't get information about colour from the retina's cones) due to the retina's rods not working properly. Causes include ageing, slow regeneration of visual purple pigment from a lack of vitamin A and beta-carotene (which the body makes into vitamin A), and an inherited eye condition called retinitis pigmentosa. Ordinary eye tests don't pick it up.

How light and colour can help

1. Glasses with lenses to help focus light clarify images and prevent dazzle.

2. Eat plenty of foods rich in beta-carotene. And within the bounds of a healthy diet, eat more foods rich in vitamin A (butter, whole- and half-fat milk, eggs, liver and kidney).

3. When driving at night, consider wearing glasses with yellow lenses to filter out potentially dangerous glare from street lights and car headlights. They may also make driving safer in rain, snow, fog, mist and haze.

Doctors or optometrists may also recommend tests with the Pelli-Robson chart (a modified version of the usual Snellen letter chart), which has letters of decreasing blackness.

Short sight

Short-sighted (myopic or near-sighted) eyeballs are long from front to back, making distant objects look fuzzy because their images are focused in front of the retina.

How light and colour can help

1. Look away from close work every few minutes and focus on something far away.

2. Several times a day, rest and darken the eyes by 'palming' – covering them with your palms for 1–3 minutes.

3. Visit an optometrist or ophthalmologist for advice on glasses or contact lenses.

4. Consider wearing individually shaped, hard plastic contact lenses all night or for a few hours by day. Their pressure changes the shape of the cornea, making the eyeball shorter. New lenses are needed as the eye shape changes. Details from the British Orthokeratology Society (see page 156).

5. Consider wearing pinhole glasses for 30 minutes a day.

6. Discuss with your doctor a laser treatment called laser refractive surgery. This shaves the central area of the cornea to reduce the length of the eye. The two types – photorefractive keratectomy (PRK) and laser in situ keratomileusis (LASIK) – are suitable for different people.

7. For severe visual impairment, contact the UK's Royal National Institute for the Blind (see page 157) for practical information and support.

8. One small study of a group of 20 children with visual impairment in both eyes found a striking improvement in their vision when they wore yellow lenses with very little vision-correcting power. There is no good proof that this works, but you can test it by looking at a distant object through a yellow acetate gel sheet.

9. Consider having flashing-light therapy to stimulate the vision in a 'lazy' eye.

Other tips

Remove glasses or contact lenses and do these exercises:

● Morning and evening, splash closed eyes 20 times with warm water, then 20 times with cold. This increases the eyes' circulation and nutrient supply.

● Once a day, for 30 seconds, put your forefinger 15–25cm (6–10in) from your eyes, then move your head as you watch your finger 'moving' from side to side; repeat, watching the background instead of your finger. Repeat. This helps the eyes adjust to different focal lengths.

Doctors may also recommend surgery called radial keratotomy to reduce the cornea's thickness.

Long sight

Since longsighted (hypermetropic) eyeballs are short from front to back, images of nearby objects are focused behind the retina and perceived as fuzzy.

How light and colour can help

1. Illuminate close work well.

2. Arrange for the source of light to be behind your left shoulder if you are right-handed and your right one if left-handed.

3. Accustom the eyes to close work by starting off with larger print.

4. Several times a day remove glasses or contact lenses, and rest the eyes by 'palming' – covering them with your palms for 1–3 minutes.

5. Try using pinhole glasses (see Trayner glasses, page 157), building up from five to 30 minutes a day.

6. Visit your optometrist or ophthalmologist for advice on glasses or contact lenses.

7. Discuss with your doctor the pros and cons of laser surgery (PRK or LASIK, see Short Sight, above) to shave the outer edges of the cornea.

Other tips

● Try the exercises described under Short sight, above, without glasses or contact lenses.

Far sight

Far sight (presbyopia) stops us seeing near things clearly. In our 40s, 50s or 60s our 'near point' – the comfortable distance between the eyes and close work – moves further away, probably because the eyes' lenses grow larger as we age. This puts pressure on the ciliary muscles so they become lax and can't tighten properly to make the lens fatter when viewing close things.

How light and colour can help

1. Illuminate close work well.
2. Sit so that the light source comes from behind your left shoulder if right-handed and your right if left-handed.
3. Change focus frequently by looking up from close work and concentrating on something a long way away.
4. Discuss wearing glasses or contact lenses with your optometrist or ophthalmologist.
5. Nourish your eyes' lenses with a healthy diet, including plenty of foods rich in vitamin C and flavonoids.
6. Exercise regularly to keep the arteries which supply the eyes with nutrients healthy.
7. Try pinhole glasses.

Astigmatism

This results from the cornea being unevenly curved, so that vision is not uniformly clear.

How light and colour can help

1. An optometrist or ophthalmologist can advise on glasses, or on contact lenses (including ones that change the shape of the cornea – details from the British Orthokeratology Society, see page 156).
2. Ask your doctor about laser treatment to smooth the cornea.

Cataract

This is a loss of lens translucency that makes things look fuzzy and, for some types of cataract, yellowish or reddish. Estimating distances may be difficult too.

Healthy lenses need to be in antioxidant-rich fluid; ageing reduces the volume of this fluid, and the concentrations of antioxidant plant pigments called lutein and zeaxanthin in the lens and fluid; being overweight may also reduce antioxidant concentration. All this encourages oxidation of clear lens proteins (crystallins) by free radicals, induced by stresses such as over-exposure to UV, and smoking. Cataracts are more likely in sunny countries, and smoking more than 20 cigarettes a day triples the risk.

Other risk factors include high blood pressure, uncontrolled or poorly controlled diabetes, eye injury or infection, certain medications (such as inhaled steroids, and pilocarpine eyedrops), a family history of cataracts, schizophrenia (whether from medication, a poor diet, or something else is unclear), and poor growth before or after birth.

How light and colour can help

1. Stay inside or in the shade on a bright sunny summer's day from 11am-3pm, or wear UV-filtering sunglasses, prescription glasses or contact lenses.

2. Get some bright daylight at other times, since lenses clouded by cataracts reduce light stimulation of the hypothalamus and may cause depression and sleep problems.

3. Use a UV-free light visor or box early in the morning to help correct a disrupted body clock.

4. Eat more foods rich in eye-friendly antioxidant plant pigments – proanthocyanidins, beta-carotene, lutein and zeaxanthin. Consider taking bilberry extract twice daily.

5. Cook tomatoes in fat to release more lycopene. This, plus zeaxanthin, helps prevent blue light damaging the eyes' lenses.

Other tips

● To reduce free-radical damage, avoid smoking and breathing smoky or polluted air.

● To counteract oxidation, eat at least five daily helpings of vegetables and fruit, and plenty of foods rich in vitamins B, C and E, quercetin, and salicylates (which resemble aspirin).

● Consider taking food supplements of vitamins C and E, or quercetin, especially if your diet is poor.

● Lose excess weight, as being overweight 'dilutes' the antioxidants available to your lenses (unless you take a supplement). Fat around the waist is particularly associated with a higher risk of cataracts.

Doctors may also recommend, if you are on a 'cataractogenic' drug, reducing your dose or taking an alternative. A small daily dose of aspirin may prevent cataracts worsening. Cataract removal and the implantation of an artificial lens is usually performed under local anaesthesia, without stitches.

Age-related macular degeneration (AMD)

This difficulty in seeing colour and fine detail is due to degeneration in the macula, the pinhead-sized yellow spot in the middle of the retina. 'Dry' AMD, the usual type, means the pigmented layer of the retina and some photoreceptors degenerate because of a build-up of waste products. The more serious 'wet' AMD means abnormal blood vessels form under the retina due to a poor supply of nutrients and poor clearance of waste. These vessels leak and can cause scarring.

The causes include ageing, high blood pressure for sight, and oxidation due to free radicals induced by stresses such as smoking and, probably, obesity, diabetes and over-exposure to UV. Having light-coloured eyes may make it, or cataracts, more likely. High levels of the plant pigments lutein and zeaxanthin in the macula help protect against UV damage by absorbing UV; they also act as antioxidants.

How light and colour can help

1. Stay inside from 11am to 3pm in bright sunlight, stay in the shade, or wear UV-filtering sunglasses, prescription glasses or contact lenses.

2. Go out in bright daylight at other times each day to raise your night-time level of melatonin, a very powerful antioxidant.

3. Eat more foods rich in the antioxidant carotenoids, beta-carotene, lutein and zeaxanthin to help protect the macula.

4. Cook tomatoes in fat to release more lycopene. This, plus zeaxanthin, helps prevent damage from blue light.

5. Consider taking supplements of beta-carotene and lutein.

6. 'Wet' AMD may improve with one of two laser treatments. The first is laser photo-coagulation, destroying new blood vessels with a 'hot' laser; since this creates a permanent blind spot it is unsuitable if the vessels are under the macula. The second is photo-dynamic therapy. Used early, this may halt progression. A photosensitive dye (verteporfin) is injected into an arm vein and taken up by the new vessels. A 'cold' low-intensity laser shone in the eye for five minutes activates the dye, destroying the vessels. You need four to six treatments in the first year and must avoid bright light for 48 hours after each one.

Other tips

● Stop smoking to reduce further damage; if necessary, get help from your doctor, a counsellor or Quitline (see Open Your Eyes to Working with VDUs, page 157).

● Eat more foods rich in antioxidants (vitamins C and E, selenium and zinc) to reduce further damage.

● Lose excess weight, as being overweight 'dilutes' the antioxidants available to your retinas.

● Consider taking supplements of vitamins C and E, selenium, lutein and zeaxanthin, and the herbal remedies *Ginkgo biloba* and bilberry extract.

Doctors may also recommend an operation called macular translocation, which restores a healthy retina in some people.

Lungs and breathing

Snoring

The noise generally comes from vibration of the soft palate. Being overweight and having a fat neck encourage it. The noise doesn't usually perturb the snorer but is difficult for others to ignore, especially if it varies in volume and regularity. Some snorers have periodic interruptions to their breathing lasting many seconds, called apnoea ('stop-breathing') attacks. The snore or snort on starting to breathe again may make a much louder noise than usual. More seriously, people who suffer from apnoea attacks have an increased risk of heart disease.

How light and colour can help

A doctor can use a laser beam as a scalpel to shave away a thin portion of tissue from along the edge of the soft palate. While not always successful, this makes a big difference to some people's snoring.

Other tips

● Position yourself at night so you can easily breathe through your nose, not your mouth.
● Sleep on your side, not your back.
● Lose excess weight.
● Don't smoke or take sedatives, and avoid alcohol after 6pm.
● A snorer's partner could try blotting out the sounds at night by wearing earplugs or listening to a tape of soothing music through headphones. Although this is unlikely to keep you awake if it plays all night, there is a newly marketed gadget called the Sound Spa that plays for 60 minutes and then turns itself off.
● Although unproven, it wouldn't hurt to try singing for five minutes or more each day – and it might help. Especially if you are overweight, using your mouth and throat muscles this way may reduce the amount of fat deposited among the muscle fibres. And this could increase the amount of space available for air to pass through the back of your throat during sleep.

Doctors or dentists may also recommend checking for any nasal obstruction such as lumps called polyps, or the inflammatory swelling of allergic rhinitis ('hay fever'). An individually made dental appliance may help keep the airway clear by bringing the lower jaw forward at night. A CPAP (continuous positive airway pressure) pump helps prevent apnoea attacks by trickling a continuous stream of air through a mask as a person sleeps. Ask your doctor for details.

Tuberculosis (TB)

This infection with *Mycobacterium tuberculosis* bacteria generally attacks the lungs, though can infect lymph nodes ('glands', for example, in the neck), bone, skin and certain other parts of the body too. It is much less common than it used to be, but can still occur in people living in close quarters, especially if their resistance is low – for example, if they are elderly, or have diabetes, cancer, AIDS or another long-term illness, or are on steroid medication. TB is no longer a rare illness and is on the increase.

How light and colour can help

1. Exposure to sunlight (taking care not to burn) makes TB of the skin less likely.
2. UV light can also help treat TB of the skin.
3. Exposure to sunlight helps cure TB anywhere else. However, it's been noted that sunlight doesn't help if sunglasses are worn, which raises the possibility that the beneficial effects of UV, and other rays in sunshine, act via light activation of parts of the brain rather than simply through the skin.
4. Visualize white cells engulfing TB bacteria.

Other tips

● Boost your resistance by eating foods rich in beta-carotene, vitamins C and E, selenium, zinc and plant pigments.
● Get up and move around if you are well enough, otherwise do arm and shoulder exercises several times a day to boost your circulation and aid healing.

Doctors also recommend antibiotics, but there is an increasing problem with the body's resistance to these drugs. It's very important to trace people you've been in contact with, so they can be screened for TB.

Blood, blood vessels, and heart

Anaemia

Mild iron-deficiency anaemia causes few, if any, problems. Severe anaemia can cause fatigue, paleness, breathlessness, a sore tongue, sore corners of the mouth, and thin, brittle, spoon-shaped nails. Causes include a poor diet, bleeding, or poor digestion or absorption of food.

How light and colour can help

Some colour therapists advise bathing the legs in red light, and the left upper abdomen in orange light, and some advocate breathing air lit with red light. They claim this breaks down iron salts in the body, releasing ferric ions that are more easily used to make haemoglobin. These treatments lack scientific evidence. However, you'll lose nothing by getting more exposure to sunlight (taking care not to burn), or even bathing in red light (from a red light bulb, or a bulb shielded with a red gel sheet), for 30 minutes a day.

Other tips

● Eat more foods containing iron, and vitamin C and copper, both of which aid the absorption of iron.
● Drink orange juice (fresh, or vitamin-C-enriched) with meals, instead of coffee, tea, cola or alcohol – which reduce iron absorption.
● Consider cooking in stainless steel or non-enamel coated cast-iron pans, to raise your iron intake.
● Make meal-times relaxed.

Doctors may also recommend iron medicine.

High blood pressure (hypertension)

This can be encouraged by obesity, smoking, stress, and artery or kidney disease. Sometimes, though, there is no obvious reason. It's more likely in people who were born light, short or thin, and became overweight later. Pre-eclampsia in pregnancy encourages high blood pressure (BP) in later life. The BP tends to rise in winter and fall in summer.

High BP encourages angina, heart attacks, strokes and kidney disease in a few people. Research suggests this may be due to a low level of nitric oxide (made from arginine, found in meat, beans, peanuts, chocolate, seeds and grains). Since there is no test as yet to identify individuals at risk, experts recommend treating all high BP.

How light and colour can help

1. Go out in bright daylight, ideally sunshine, each day, as UVB helps lower high BP. It stimulates vitamin-D production, which regulates calcium and phosphorus levels in muscle cells in blood-vessel walls, and stops them tightening too much. One session can lower the BP for several days, and decrease

the systolic BP (the upper of the two numbers in a BP measurement) by an average of 17mm (³/₄in) of mercury!

2. Use full-spectrum fluorescent light.

3. Consider bathing in blue light, which acts through the eyes and the skin.

4. Use visualization to aid relaxation.

5. Eat more foods rich in proanthocyanidin plant pigments, and consider taking these as a supplement.

Other tips

● Stop smoking.

● Lose excess weight, particularly if you are 'apple-shaped'. For each 1kg (2.2lb) lost, your systolic BP (the higher of the two numbers recorded) will fall by 2.5mm (¹/₁₀th in) of mercury.

● Take a daily 30 minutes exercise. Combining exercise and weight loss lowers the BP more than either alone.

● Use effective stress management, as feeling continuously stressed raises the BP as much as an extra 20 years of age, or 18kg (40lb) of body-weight.

● Eat a healthy diet with more foods rich in vitamins B6 and C, flavonoids, potassium, magnesium, calcium and omega-3s. Avoid salted foods as these raise some people's BP. Go easy on coffee and alcohol.

● Consider supplements of calcium and magnesium (not if you have kidney disease), vitamin C, rutin, quercetin, fish oil, and the amino acids taurine and arginine.

● Consider consulting a herbalist. BP-lowering herbs include black cohosh (*Cimicifuga racemosa*), dong quai (*Angelica sinensis*), yarrow (*Achillea millefolium*) and motherwort (*Leonurus cardiaca*).

Doctors may also recommend

BP-lowering drugs if six months of natural treatments don't work, or your BP is very high.

Angina, heart attacks, 'TIAs' and strokes

Disease that narrows arteries may make them unable to supply enough blood to the heart or brain. This leads to angina (heart pain, usually on exertion), heart attacks, strokes ('brain attacks') or mini-strokes (transient ischaemic attacks or TIAs).

One cause of narrowing is a build-up of a fatty, LDL-cholesterol-rich substance called atheroma. Another is inflammation from immune-cell attack of atheroma containing oxidized LDL-cholesterol; this scars and roughens the artery's lining, encouraging a blood clot that narrows its channel further. Blood that clots too readily makes matters worse.

Risk factors include high blood pressure, obesity, diabetes, stress and depression, all of which are influenced by light, as well as an unhealthy diet, smoking, gum disease and peptic ulcers. Heart attacks and strokes are commoner in winter, when lack of UV may raise cholesterol, and cold weather makes blood clot more readily.

How light and colour can help

1. Have 30 minutes of bright outdoor daylight – preferably sunlight – each day. Its UV can

lower a high cholesterol level by up to 10 per cent; may lower triglyceride fats, which can also be important; and boosts the blood's oxygen-carrying power. It also encourages a good night-time level of antioxidant melatonin. And pleasure from sunbathing could help counteract stress-related heart disease.

2. Have bright indoor lighting to reduce depression and anxiety.

3. Consider regular sunbed sessions.

4. After a heart attack, convalesce in a bright, sunny room. This encourages survival, possibly by raising the spirits and reducing depression.

5. Use visualization to aid relaxation.

6. Eat more foods rich in beta-carotene and flavonoid plant pigments, and use more turmeric.

7. Some vascular surgeons use laser light to clear blocked arteries.

Other tips

● Stop smoking.

● Treat high blood pressure.

● Lose excess weight.

● Eat plenty of foods rich in fibre, vitamins C and E, salicylates and essential fatty acids, and spice food with ginger. This helps prevent atheroma, helps prevent low-density lipoprotein cholesterol (LDL-C) being changed to its dangerous form – oxidized LDL-C – and helps prevent inflammation.

● Consider taking supplements of vitamin E.

● Learn to manage stress, depression and anger more effectively.

Doctors may also recommend medications such as aspirin to reduce the risk of clots, and statins to lower cholesterol. An angioplasty procedure widens a narrowed coronary artery, while a bypass graft operation bypasses it. A shock from a defibrillator can save life after a heart attack. A heart transplant is a last resort, though scientists are working on an artificial 'bionic' heart.

Digestive system

Tooth decay

Decay results mainly from eating foods containing added sugar. Mouth bacteria break down sugar and release acid within 10 minutes. This acid dissolves the surface of tooth enamel, and repeated long-lasting acid attack causes dental decay.

How light and colour can help

1. Go out in bright daylight, preferably sunlight, each day, as UV triggers vitamin-D production in the skin, and vitamin D boosts the levels of calcium and other minerals that strengthen teeth.

2. Choose full-spectrum lighting if you work all day in electric light.

3. Researchers are working on a toothbrush that beams light onto special toothpaste containing light-sensitive compounds. Once activated, they hope these will kill the bacteria that cause decay.

Other tips

● Stop smoking.
● Brush twice daily with fluoride toothpaste to remove food residues and strengthen enamel. After food that contains added sugar, brush teeth and eat celery, apple, cheese or nuts, or rub your tongue around your mouth, then rinse with water.
● Floss to remove food residues when necessary.
● Eat foods rich in calcium and other minerals to strengthen teeth. Limit sugary foods to meal-times, when saliva flows fast and washes acid away.
● Soak a cotton bud in clove oil and place over a cavity in a tooth. Eugenol in the oil numbs exposed nerves and kills bacteria.

Dentists may also recommend lessons in effective toothbrushing, or a filling.

Jaundice in babies

Most babies who become jaundiced do so in the first day or two, and appear slightly yellow. This is nearly always 'physiological' jaundice caused by a raised level of the bile pigment bilirubin, due to the liver not yet working efficiently. It usually clears within 10 days in full-term babies, but takes longer in pre-terms ('premature' babies).

How light and colour can help

1. Bathing skin in bright blue or blue-green light from a hospital phototherapy unit each day helps clear physiological jaundice by breaking down bilirubin. Eye pads, an eye shield, or an orange head-shield must be used to protect the baby's eyes, because babies' 'young' lenses transmit more light to the retina than do those of adults.

2. Mild jaundice may respond to the blue rays in bright daylight. Avoid direct sunlight because a baby's skin lacks melanin and burns easily with UV. Researchers are also investigating the possibility that bright sunlight or electric light could damage a pre-term baby's retinas.

Other tips

● Breastfeed frequently. Give bottle-fed babies boiled water between feeds, if necessary.

Doctors may also recommend tests for infection or the abnormal breakdown of red blood cells, plus, for a two-week-old, tests for liver and thyroid disease.

Muscles

Fibromyalgia

This 'muscular rheumatism' or 'fibrositis' is muscle pain and stiffness, often with hard knots and cords in the shoulder and back muscles, as well as tenderness of at least 11 'myofascial trigger points', found:
☞ At the sides of the base of the skull.
☞ At the sides of the neck, between the fifth and seventh vertebrae.
☞ In the middle of each upper trapezius muscle (which runs between the neck and shoulder).

☞ At the end of each supraspinatus muscle (which runs along the upper edge of the shoulderblade).

☞ In each pectoral muscle, above where the second rib meets the breastbone.

☞ In each outer elbow.

☞ Deep in each buttock.

☞ Behind each hip joint, by the piriformis muscle.

☞ Inside each knee.

Other possible problems include fatigue, disturbed sleep, headaches, Raynaud's phenomenon, period pain, increased pain sensitivity, poor memory or concentration, depression, restless legs and the irritable bowel syndrome. Fibromyalgia sometimes begins after a shock, and may be affected by activity, stress, weather, and low serotonin.

How light and colour can help

1. Boost serotonin by going out for at least 30 minutes a day to get bright light in the eyes and on the skin.

2. Consider using a light visor or box (see pages 156–7) for up to two hours a day.

Other tips

● Discover the balance of rest and exercise that helps most.

● Try heat from warm baths, or alternate steam or sauna sessions with a cold shower or swim (not if you have heart disease).

● Eat foods rich in vitamin B, calcium and magnesium. Choose cabbage and lemons for their anti-inflammatory substances. Avoid refined carbohydrates (which encourage

fluid retention) and offal, yeast extract, beef, pork, chocolate, herrings, mackerel, shellfish, fish roe, sherry and port (which contain purines). Have three helpings a week of salmon or tuna for omega-3s, and because, unlike other oily fish, they are low in purines which produce muscle-irritating uric acid. Reduce caffeine-containing drinks.

● Try supplements of calcium and magnesium (to relax muscles), and 5HTP (5 hydroxytryptophan, needed for serotonin production – but not if you are on antidepressant drugs, or St John's wort).

● Use effective stress-management.

● Block pain with a TENS (trans-cutaneous electrical nerve stimulation) machine.

● Stimulate points with massage, heat, cold, liniment or acupressure to relieve tenderness and radiating pain.

Doctors may also recommend certain anti-depressants to improve sleep, non-steroidal anti-inflammatories, steroids, tranquillizers, acupuncture and osteopathy.

Muscle weakness

This can result from a lack of vitamin D due to too little sunlight; see Osteomalacia, page 131.

Bones and joints

Arthritis

Arthritis means pain and stiffness in the joints. Osteoarthritis (OA) is a roughening of a joint's surfaces caused by wear and tear. Rheumatoid arthritis (RA) is an autoimmune ('self-allergic') disease, resulting from abnormal immune-system behaviour. Possible triggers include certain foods (such as wheat, meat, dairy produce, eggs, animal fat, sugar and coffee), stress, infection, certain chemicals (such as leaking domestic gas). The Pill lowers the risk of RA, and pregnancy can improve it for up to three months after childbirth. Arthritis can also occur with gout, psoriasis, inflammatory bowel disease and certain other disorders.

How light and colour can help

1. Expose skin to more bright daylight (sunlight when possible). Its heat helps by warming the joints, and UV stimulates the production of vitamin D and oestrogen (which strengthen bone in joints), and endorphins (which reduce pain).
2. For rheumatoid arthritis, exposure of joints to bright red or blue light, perhaps polarized or low-power ('soft') laser light, soothes pain in some people.
3. Eat more foods rich in flavonoid plant pigments (especially proanthocyanidins) and beta-carotene,
4. Consider supplements of plant pigments such as beta-carotene and proanthocyanidins.

Other tips

- Avoid straining joints.
- Balance periods of rest and exercise.
- Move often to prevent stiffening.
- Build up muscles around joints with strengthening exercises.
- Ease pain with warmth, cold, or alternate heat and cold.
- Eat more raw leafy vegetables, and foods rich in essential fats, vitamins C, D and E, and selenium.
- Try to identify any suspected food sensitivities. Some people with OA, for example, react to tomatoes, potatoes, peppers and aubergines.
- Each day, drink two cups of ginger tea, two glasses of hot water with half a tablespoon of apple cider vinegar and a teaspoon of honey, and one glass of juice made from beetroots, carrots, cucumber and celery.
- Consider supplements of vitamins C, D and E, selenium and fish oil (for omega-3 fatty acids) or cod liver oil (for omega-3s and vitamins A and D (if on cod liver oil, avoid other vitamin A and D supplements) and glucosamine (an amino-sugar needed by joints).
- Avoid hyperventilating (breathing too rapidly) as this raises the body's acidity level.
- Consider consulting a medical herbalist.

Doctors may also recommend painkillers (be aware that long-term non-steroidal anti-inflammatory drugs can cause stomach ulcers). The newest treatments for RA include regular blood filtering to remove rheumatoid antibodies, and anti-tumour necrosis-factor drugs.

Osteoporosis

This makes bones thin, light and fragile. Triggers include an early menopause, absent periods from an eating disorder or habitual over-exertion, smoking, poor diet, too much alcohol, insufficient weight-bearing exercise, overly light weight, long-term steroids, cancer, a liver or thyroid disorder, and insufficient light.

Bone mineral density normally peaks in the late 20s, starts falling in the 30s, and drops faster as hormone levels decrease after the menopause. But at any age simple lifestyle measures can strengthen bones or prevent further weakening.

How light and colour can help

1. Each day go out for a while in bright daylight, preferably sunlight, as UV boosts the production of oestrogen and vitamin D, helping keep bones strong.
2. Eat more foods rich in flavonoid plant pigments.

Other tips

● Stop smoking.
● Eat more foods rich in calcium, magnesium, zinc, vitamins C and K, and plant hormones.
● Cut out added salt and sugar, and fizzy drinks, have less coffee, animal protein and processed foods, and avoid over-indulging in alcohol.
● Consider taking supplements of a multi-mineral, glucosamine (an amino-sugar) and isoflavone plant hormones.
● Take regular weight-bearing exercise, such as walking, dancing or tennis.

Doctors may also recommend after the menopause, HRT (hormone replacement therapy), raloxifene (a selective oestrogen re-uptake modulator or 'SERM' which, unlike HRT, does not increase the risk of breast cancer), or etidronate.

Rickets and osteomalacia

Rickets is the softening and bending of young bones; osteomalacia is the weakening of older bones. Both are due to poor uptake of calcium and other minerals from a lack of vitamin D. Rickets causes general illness, while osteomalacia causes fractures, bone and muscle pain, and weakness. The usual cause is a lack of daylight on the skin, which is common in elderly people who stay inside, dark-skinned people who live in very northerly or southerly countries, and anyone who keeps their legs and arms covered. It seems to be associated with cancers of the breast, colon, prostate and ovary.

How light and colour can help

1. Go outside each day in bright daylight, as UV triggers vitamin D production. Up to 30 minutes at noon two or three times a week, with bare hands, arms and face in summer is enough for an adult with skin-type 2 (see page 54), for example, to store enough vitamin D for winter. Olive-skinned or black people need more exposure because of their extra melanin.
2. Wear light-coloured clothing to let more UV through.

Other tips

Eat oily fish for vitamin D. Fortified foods such as breakfast cereals help, but the natural vitamin is best. If you can't get enough vitamin D from sunlight and your diet, take a daily supplement.

Doctors may also recommend

supplements of vitamin D and, perhaps, calcium.

Sex, fertility and reproductive organs

Low sex drive

Psychological causes include lack of attraction or privacy; discomfort; depression; fear of pregnancy, pain, failure, criticism or lack of control; disinterest if pregnancy isn't possible; poor sexual self-esteem; and previous sexual abuse. Physical causes include an underactive thyroid, arterial disease, diabetes, anorexia, other illness, inebriation, hormone deficiency, ageing and certain drugs. Behavioural causes include a lack of foreplay, a lack of practice at sex, and masturbation.

How light and colour can help

1. Get more bright outdoor daylight on your skin and in your eyes. This will increase your production of sex hormones, endorphins and serotonin, which may give you a 'feel-good' boost and make you feel more sexual.
2. Use bright indoor lighting.
3. Consider using a light visor or box (see pages 156–7).

Other tips

● Take regular exercise to increase hormone levels.
● Eat more foods rich in vitamins B and E, zinc and plant hormones. Include brown rice and whole rye or wheat grains (for histidine, an amino acid that aids sexual arousal).
● Consider a supplement of vitamin-B complex.
● Consider herbal remedies such as ginseng, *Avena sativa* (wild oats), dong kwai, catuaba, schizandra, *Muira puama* or astragalus.
● Put three drops of ylang ylang, jasmine (not if pregnant or breastfeeding), benzoin, ginger, sandalwood or rose oil in bath water.
● Have a sensual massage, using three drops of any two of the above oils in two teaspoons of sweet almond oil. Alternatively, massaging your partner may be exciting.

Doctors may also recommend hormone
replacement therapy in later life.

Pre-menstrual syndrome (PMS)

From a week ot two before your period, until a few days after it starts, you may feel irritable, depressed, forgetful, hungry (especially for carbohydrates), dizzy, tired and faint; you may also sleep badly, and have fluid retention, headaches and palpitations, and painful joints and muscles. This probably results from over-sensitivity to progesterone, plus a body-clock disturbance that causes imbalances of ovarian hormones and neurotransmitters (such as serotonin and GABA – gamma-amino butyric acid).

How light and colour can help

1. Get more bright daylight, preferably outside, each day.
2. Bathe in bright light from a light visor or box each day.
3. Wear a mask that flashes red light for 15 minutes a day. Start with 30 flashes a second, adjusting it if necessary from 8 to 50. This helps three in four women, probably by resetting the body clock and raising endorphin levels. It is the most effective therapy. You may be able to do without it for 7-10 days after your period starts.

Other tips

● Exercise each day.
● Use effective stress management.
● Have a daily massage with two drops each of lavender, rose and geranium oils in two tablespoons of sweet almond oil.
● Eat small, regular meals, with more foods rich in chromium, iron, magnesium, zinc, vitamins A, B, C and E, plant hormones, and a good balance of omega-3 and omega-6 fatty acids. Have high-carbohydrate, low-protein snacks of foods rich in the amino acid

tryptophan (bananas, cauliflower, potatoes, nuts, dates, pumpkin seeds and wholegrains). Have less salt, alcohol and caffeine.
● Consider supplements of vitamin B6, calcium, magnesium, evening primrose oil and isoflavone plant hormones.
● Have a warm sitz bath every other day for two weeks before a period. This means sitting in a large container of cold water, with feet in warm water, for 10 minutes.
● Consider a daily dose of a hormone-balancing herb such as chasteberry (*Vitex agnus castus)* or black cohosh (*Cimicifuga racemosa*). Continue for three months, but avoid if on the Pill, HRT or other hormones, or if pregnant.
● Consider taking St John's wort.

Doctors may also recommend SSRI (selective serotonin-reuptake inhibitor – antidepressants that boost the availability of serotonin), the Pill or diuretics.

Heavy periods

Causes include a poor diet, stress, food sensitivity, an underactive thyroid, certain drugs, smoking, an oestrogen-dominant hormone imbalance, fibroids, polyps, infection, a coil, endometriosis in the womb's wall, pelvic inflammatory disease, anaemia, a blood-clotting disorder and womb cancer. Some 'heavy periods' are miscarriages.

How light and colour can help

1. Get more bright light each day to help correct any hormone imbalance.

2. Researchers are investigating the use of photodynamic therapy (see page 104).

3. As a last resort, consider having your womb lining removed (endometrial ablation). This is done under local anaesthetic with a laser beam (or microwaves, heat or radio waves).

Other tips

● Eat more foods rich in calcium, magnesium, zinc and plant hormones, including lignans (in sunflower and sesame seeds, cracked linseeds, wholegrains, beans and peas), and have a good balance of omega-3 and omega-6 fatty acids (most people have too much omega-6 and too little omega-3). Eat less meat but more citrus fruit. Cinnamon and thyme may help.

● Identify any suspected food sensitivity.

● Have a daily tummy massage using three drops each of geranium, cypress and rose oils in two teaspoons of sweet almond oil.

Doctors may also recommend a non-steroidal anti-inflammatory drug, a progestogen-releasing coil, removal of a coil, the combined Pill (the kind that contains both oestrogen and progesterone), hormone replacement therapy, endometrial ablation (see above) or – as a last resort – hysterectomy.

Irregular periods

Regular periods require regular ovulation, which requires a good balance of hormones from the hypothalamus, pituitary and ovaries. Irregular ovulation is normal for several years after menstruation first starts, before the menopause and while breastfeeding. It is often associated with infertility.

The triggers include rapid weight loss, being very underweight, having an oestrogen-dominant hormone imbalance (caused, for example, by bingeing or being obese), vitamin B deficiency, anaemia, diabetes and an overactive thyroid. Other possibilties include sex hormone disruption associated with a raised melatonin level due to short winter days, and disruption to the body clock by long-haul air travel. Other culprits include certain medications (including the Pill and some blood-pressure lowering medication), moving in with another woman (though periods synchronize over several months), stopping the Pill, and damage to ovarian arteries by sterilization. Up to nine women in 10 also have polycystic ovaries. Bleeding between periods (for example, from fibroids, polyps, certain ovarian cysts, pelvic inflammatory disease or cervix or womb cancer) may mimic irregular periods.

How light and colour can help

1. If hormone tests, or an ovulation monitor, reveal irregular or absent ovulation, encourage regular ovulation by spending more time in bright light – preferably outdoors, though bright electric light could help too.

2. Use brighter electric light in the evening.

3. Consider using a light visor or box in the morning or evening.

4. Consider a six-month trial of sleeping at night with a 100-watt light switched on from days 14–17 of your cycle.

Other tips

● Eat more foods rich in plant hormones (to balance hormone levels), vitamin B (if feeling stressed) and vitamin E. Encourage a healthy hormone balance by aiming to eat a good balance of omega-3 and omega-6 fatty acids (probably less omega-6). If you are overweight or tend to binge, counteract a high oestrogen level by eating less fat, especially saturated fat, and more fibre.

● Consider taking supplements of vitamins B and E, and isoflavone plant hormones.

● If hormone tests show a low progesterone level after ovulation, take a three-month course of chasteberry (*Vitex agnus castus*), with a dose each morning, starting on the first day of a period. If you aren't ovulating, take a dose of false unicorn root (*Chamaelirium luteum*) twice daily. Alternatively, for unexplained irregular periods, take a dose of tincture containing both herbs each morning, or consult a medical herbalist for personalized advice. (Don't take *Vitex* if on the Pill, HRT or other hormones; under-20s should take *Vitex* only if advised by a medical herbalist.)

● Soak in bath water containing two drops each of rose, geranium and lavender oils. Or add the same amounts to two teaspoons of sweet almond oil for a massage. These oils aid relaxation and hormone balance.

● Occasionally, irregular bleeding results from womb cancer, so see your doctor for tests if you bleed after sex, between periods or after the menopause.

● See your doctor if you haven't had a period by the age of 16 or 17.

Doctors may also recommend the progestogen-only Pill, progesterone pessaries (but not cream, as progesterone isn't absorbed well from this) or an ovulation-stimulating drug called clomiphene.

Polycystic ovaries

Multiple small cysts in the ovaries come and go within hours or days, and result from an imbalance of oestrogen or other hormones from fat cells or the ovaries, hypothalamus or the pituitary or adrenal glands. This imbalance can cause the polycystic ovary syndrome (PCOS), perhaps with acne, excess body hair, thinning head hair, infrequent or absent periods, infertility, an early menopause and a raised risk of womb cancer. Possible triggers include stress, obesity and bingeing. Most women with bulimia have polycystic ovaries, and one woman in three with PCOS often binges. Also, cells tend to be resistant to the action of insulin, a hormone that enables cells to use sugar. This leads to a high blood-sugar level, a low cell-sugar level, and an increased risk of diabetes and arterial disease.

How light and colour can help

1. More exposure to bright outdoor daylight or, preferably, sunlight, may help by balancing hormones.

2. If you are overweight, suffer from winter depression or often binge on carbohydrates, have more bright light, outdoors and indoors, brighten the electric lighting, and consider using a light visor or box.

Other tips

● Help balance hormones with regular exercise, better stress-management and sustained weight loss, if necessary.

● Eat regularly, favouring foods rich in plant hormones, chromium, magnesium, zinc and fibre. Avoid high-glycaemic-index foods or eat them with foods with a low glycaemic index; eat less saturated fat; and have a good balance of omega-3 and omega-6 fatty acids.

● Consider consulting a medical herbalist to help balance your hormones. Potentially helpful herbs include false unicorn root (*Chamaelirium luteum*) – for plant oestrogens to counteract a high oestrogen level without suppressing ovulation; black cohosh (*Cimicifuga racemosa*) – particularly if stressed; and liquorice (*Glycyrrhiza glabra*) or sarsaparilla (*Smilax*, wild liquorice) for acne and excess hair.

Doctors may also recommend cyproterone acetate for excess body hair; the combined Pill; and clomiphene or electrical stimulation to trigger ovulation.

Endometriosis

Patches of womb-lining cells stray from the womb and settle on the ovaries, womb, cervix, bladder or bowel, or in the wall of the womb. Monthly bleeding then leads to inflammation and scarring, which can cause pain and, perhaps, fertility and other problems.

One suggested cause is leaking menstrual blood which contains womb-lining cells. It's normal for a little blood to flow up the fallopian tubes and be absorbed in the abdomen or pelvis, but with endometriosis it isn't absorbed. It's possible that sex during a period encourages retrograde flow. An oestrogen-dominant hormone imbalance makes bleeding from endometriosis patches more troublesome; immune-cell attack encourages inflammation; and the Pill may increase the risk. Endometriosis generally improves during and for some years after pregnancy, and after the menopause.

How light and colour can help

The destruction of patches of endometriosis using a laser beam is an increasingly popular medical treatment.

Other tips

● Use sanitary towels, not tampons. A tampon may not absorb the menstrual flow fast enough to allow good drainage from the womb, possibly forcing menstrual blood through the fallopian tubes.

● Avoid sex during a period, as the pressure of the penis could encourage blood to flow out of the fallopian tubes.

● Take regular exercise.

● Eat more foods rich in vitamins B, C and E, magnesium, flavonoids, salicylates, plant hormones, fibre and a good balance of omega-3 and omega-6 fatty acids to counteract inflammation. Include vegetables of the cabbage family, and bitter foods and drinks such as watercress, chicory, young dandelion leaves, rosemary and tonic water to reduce oestrogen. Cut out refined carbo-hydrates to lessen inflammation.

● Manage stress effectively to reduce pain and inflammation.

● Relieve pain with a warm bath, covered hot-water bottle, hot compress or electrically heated pad.

● Massage your tummy with warmed oil (three drops of lavender oil in three teaspoons of sweet almond oil) to ease pain.

● Drink a cup of ginger tea twice a day to help relieve inflammation.

● Consider consulting a medical herbalist. Or, twice a day, and for no longer than three months (and not if taking hormones), take a teaspoon of herbal tincture. Good choices are peony (*Paeonia lactiflora*), to reduce oestrogen and relieve pain; dandelion root (*Taraxacum officinale*) to reduce oestrogen; dong quai (*Angelica sinensis*) to balance hormones; and feverfew (*Tanacetum parthenium*) to reduce inflammation.

Doctors may also recommend

drugs such as the combined Pill or progestogens to counteract oestrogen or reduce or prevent menstruation, or drugs such as danazol to prevent pituitary stimulation of the ovaries. Surgery is sometimes recommended.

Fertility problems

Female causes can result from being over- or underweight, not having sex around ovulation, smoking, stress, too much exercise, a poor diet, sensitivity to gluten, repeated miscarriages, the polycystic ovary syndrome, blocked fallopian tubes and endometriosis. Male causes can result from

too few sperm, sperm of poor quality (sometimes due to smoking or stress), a low sex drive and erection problems (perhaps from stress or arterial disease). A lack of bright light in winter can inhibit ovulation in women and reduce sperm formation in men.

How light and colour can help

1. Relax outside in bright daylight, preferably sunlight, for 30 minutes a day to counteract stress, promote a normal hormone balance and encourage regular ovulation.

2. Consider using a light visor or box in the morning or evening.

3. Use brighter electric light in the evening.

Other tips

● Have sex two or three times a week as the timing of ovulation is unpredictable, even if periods are regular.

For women

● Use an ovulation predictor kit, and have sex some time from 72 hours before ovulation to 36 hours after. The average woman is most fertile on days 10–15. An egg must be fertilized within 24–36 hours, and sperms usually survive up to 72 hours.

● Have sex daily on waking in the week before ovulation, as most women ovulate in the afternoon and conception is more likely if sperms arrive first.

● Aim for an orgasm, as this helps sperms reach the egg; lying on the back with hips on a pillow for 30 minutes after sex also helps.

● Consider taking evening primrose oil, and a multi-mineral and vitamin supplement specially formulated for the pre-conception months.

● If over 30, seek medical help after having regular, frequent sex for a year; if over 35, do so after six months.

For men and women

● Lose excess weight.

● Take regular exercise.

● Stop smoking.

● Use effective stress-management.

● Limit alcohol, as too much depresses testosterone and encourages early miscarriage.

● Eat foods rich in beta carotene, vitamins B, C and E, folic acid, manganese (wholegrains, green leafy vegetables, pulses and nuts), selenium and zinc, to help nourish eggs and sperm.

Doctors may also recommend

drugs (gonadotrophin or clomiphene) to stimulate ovulation. For frequent early miscarriage due to the antiphospholipid syndrome (when antibodies create small blood clots in the placenta), aspirin and perhaps heparin. Surgery can sometimes unblock tubes, and destroy patches of endometriosis. Other possibilites include test-tube fertilization techniques.

Brain, mind and nerves

Anxiety

The causes include stress, certain foods which influence neurotransmitters or lower blood sugar, and a poor diet that doesn't nourish the brain properly.

How light and colour can help

1. Go outside daily in bright light to boost endorphins and help balance neurotransmitters such as serotonin.

2. Consider using a light visor or box.

3. See whether wearing clothes or choosing flowers of a particular colour is soothing. If habitually anxious, choose soothing decor colours. Aura-Soma may help, too.

4. Consider boosting relaxation by wearing a red-flashing light mask for up to 30 minutes a day. A frequency of 13 cycles per second has been found useful for post-traumatic stress.

5. Use visualization to aid relaxation.

Other tips

● Avoid too much alcohol, bingeing or other damaging 'solutions'.

● Eat more foods rich in vitamins B and E, calcium and magnesium. Steady your blood's sugar level with wholegrains, foods made with wholegrain flour (such as wholemeal bread), pulses, fruit, vegetables, nuts and seeds. Boost serotonin with a high-carbohydrate, low-protein snack that's rich in tryptophan (such as wholemeal bread, bananas, dates, hazelnuts, pumpkin seeds, and beans). Avoid too much protein, and caffeine-containing drinks.

● Drink several cups of chamomile or lemon balm tea a day.

● Exercise regularly.

● Learn to manage stress more effectively.

● Choose the flower essences whose descriptions best match how you feel, as identifying emotions can be the first step to recovery.

Doctors may also recommend

tranquillizers, to be used only temporarily.

Depression

Triggers include illness, loss, stress, an underactive thyroid, a poor diet, food sensitivity, PMS, post-natal depression, winter depression or SAD, and loneliness. Depression is linked with an imbalance of brain neurotransmitters (such as serotonin and dopamine), or a disturbance in their use. Men make serotonin faster than do women, which may help explain why women get depressed more easily.

How light and colour can help

1. Get at least 30 minutes of bright daylight each day; older people need longer. This helps balance neurotransmitters and alter the way the body responds to serotonin. Daylight's UV also stimulates an underactive thyroid.

2. Use brighter light indoors.

3. Tackle winter depression (SAD) by using a light visor or box, preferably in the early

morning, to help reset a disrupted body clock. The light intensity should be at least 2,500 lux. This helps up to four in five people within three to five days, and is often more effective than antidepressants.

4. Pay attention to the colour of clothes or flowers; this may help you to recognize underlying emotions, or give you pleasure. Aura-Soma may be useful, too.

5. Raise your spirits with colourful meals.

6. Try visualization: imagining yourself feeling better.

Other tips

● Take 30 minutes' daily exercise to boost 'feel-good' endorphins.

● Eat nutritious, attractive, regular meals rich in vitamins B (including folic acid) and C, calcium, iron, magnesium, zinc and a good balance of omega-3 and omega-6 fatty acids (most of us have too much omega-6). Avoid refined carbohydrates, which give a short-lived 'high' from serotonin and endorphins, then lead to low levels; and eat enough fat, as too little reduces cholesterol so much that brain cells can't use serotonin. The brain also needs an amino acid called tryptophan to make serotonin: boost your level with baked potatoes, bread, beans, hazelnuts, pumpkin seeds, dates, bananas and honey. Identify any suspected food sensitivity. And consider taking a multi-vitamin and mineral supplement, and fish oil.

● For mild to moderate depression, take a twice-daily dose of St John's wort (but check with your doctor if you are on drugs, or pregnant, trying to get pregnant, or breastfeeding). This makes serotonin and two other neurotransmitters, noradrenaline and dopamine, more available to nerves. But since it makes the skin more sensitive to UV, and its hypericin reacts with light to create free radicals that can encourage cataracts, protect your skin and eyes in sunlight.

● Choose flower essences whose descriptions match your feelings; identifying emotions can be the first step to recovery.

● Use aromatherapy oils.

● Have a warm bath or shower for 10 minutes, then a quick cold shower, and then repeat, to help lift your spirits

● Work with a friend or counsellor to uncover what makes you feel low, what you can do, and how to manage your reactions effectively.

● Make yourself laugh and smile; unless you are severely depressed, this should make you feel more like laughing and smiling sponta-neously.

● Do things you used to like. At the end of each day, jot down the good things that have happened, however small.

● See a doctor for severe or long-lasting depression.

Doctors may also recommend anti-depressant drugs; SSRIs (selective serotonin reuptake inhibitors) are particularly useful for winter depression.

Alzheimer's disease

This is one of many types of dementia, a condition that usually starts in old age with memory loss and progresses to personality and behaviour changes, loss of language and

mobility, and incontinence. Alzheimer's disease accounts for half of all cases of dementia; this can begin before 40, and is associated with two changes in the brain – the presence of an abnormal protein and of tangles of nerve fibres. One person in five who has dementia has the 'multi-infarct' type that is due to a series of strokes, each of which damages a part of the brain. Another type, Lewy-body dementia, is associated with shaking and hallucinations, and affects one person in six with dementia.

Since caring can be physically and emotionally arduous, it's essential to know what help is available. This may include specialist assessment and the creation of a treatment plan, information on caring and looking after yourself, support groups, financial advice, sitting by trained carers, residential respite care and nursing and medical services.

A surprising number of people with dementia stay indoors all day. Indeed, researchers who compared elderly people with Alzheimer's with healthy people of similar ages found those with Alzheimer's had only half as much daylight. This is worrying. The lack of bright light may help explain why researchers have found that people with Alzheimer's have low levels of melatonin; they also have relatively few nerve cells connecting their retinas with the pineal gland. One important result is that their body clock is very frequently out of rhythm, so they sleep badly and often wander about at night in a confused state. Their poor sleep probably goes hand in hand

with a reduction in dreaming, or REM (rapid eye movement) sleep, which is when the brain should be sorting and filing their daily experiences. Not surprisingly, all this makes them feel worse. And it makes looking after them very challenging.

How light and colour can help

1. Encourage and enable a person with Alzheimer's to spend at least an hour or so a day outside in bright light.

2. Consider trying bright light therapy with a light box each morning.

3. Researchers are experimenting to see whether taking a daily dose of melatonin before going to bed at night helps to deepen sleep.

4. Enliven the person's minute-by-minute experience of everyday life by providing plenty of colour – in their clothing and food, for example, and in the objects and backgrounds around them. Even a small thing like painting the nails of a woman with dementia can provide her with a focus of enjoyment or surprise that will be repeated over and over again, thanks to her poor short-term memory.

Other tips

● There are many causes of dementia other than Alzheimer's disease. Some, like a lack of vitamin B, an underactive thyroid, a brain tumour and alcohol or barbiturate poisoning, are reversible. Although these reversible causes are rare, it's vital to test for them early so as to rule them out.

● Those who care for someone with

Alzheimer's or any other dementia need plenty of practical support and time off. They may need emotional support too, for often such a carer is closely related – perhaps being the child or partner – and watching a loved parent, partner or other relative decline can cause immense sadness, frustration and, at times anger.

● When caring for someone with dementia, aim to provide plenty of stimulation, which can improve the memory. Music, for example, may encourage memories to surface by making people more aroused and providing a focus for their attention.

Doctors may also recommend treatment with a new drug, galantamine, developed from daffodils. This may be useful for at least one person in three. However, it's expensive, not all that helpful for improving memory and independence, and can have a lot of side effects.

Disruption due to shift work

Working on shifts – for example, in hospitals, on emergency service switchboards, or driving a lorry – can disrupt the body clock. This can reduce immunity to infection and cause sleeping problems, leaving a person tired and unwell. Many night-shift workers crave 'catnaps' when on duty; scientists are concerned that workers may be less accurate, less productive and less safe than day-workers; and there's also some suggestion that they are more prone to heart disease.

How light and colour can help

1. After a night shift, reduce your exposure to daylight before going to bed in the morning, wearing sunglasses if necessary.

2. When you get up in the afternoon, be sure to go outside for at least one hour in bright daylight. This should help you feel more alert when working that night.

3. Alternatively, use bright light from a light visor or box at the start of your 'day' to stop you feeling sleepy later.

4. Have a 'light break' in a very brightly lit room, or in front of a light box, to help keep you awake on night duty.

Jet-lag

This results from body-clock disruption due to crossing time zones by air. Flying eastwards is usually worst. It takes at least one day per hour lost or gained for your body clock to readjust naturally. Until then you may be tired, slow, clumsy and irritable, feel cold, and sleep badly. This is partly due to changes in the levels of melatonin and other hormones. Frequent jet-lag in long-haul aircrew is associated with an increase in the risk of breast cancer.

How light and colour can help

1. When travelling west, delay your body clock to put off the time you feel ready for bed by going out in bright daylight. If it is dark outside, use very bright domestic lighting, or use a light visor or box for the time recommended with the product. Do this between the following times:

If you've had a:

4-hour time-zone shift	1800–2400 hours
8-hour time-zone shift	1400–2000 hours
12-hour time-zone shift	1000–1600 hours

Encourage adjustment by avoiding bright light (by staying in or wearing dark glasses) between the following times:

If you've had a:

4-hour time-zone shift	0100–0700 hours
8-hour time-zone shift	2100–0300 hours
12-hour time-zone shift	1700–2300 hours

2. When travelling east, advance your body clock to help adjust to your earlier bedtime by using bright light. If it is dark outside, use very bright domestic lighting, or use a light visor or box. Do this between the following times:

If you've had a:

4-hour time-zone shift	0900	1500 hours
8-hour time-zone shift	1300	1900 hours
12-hour time-zone shift	1000	1600 hours

Encourage adjustment by avoiding bright light (by staying in or wearing dark glasses) between the following times:

If you've had a:

4-hour time-zone shift	0200	0800 hours
8-hour time-zone shift	0600	1200 hours
12-hour time-zone shift	1700	2300 hours

Other tips

● On arrival, go to bed and get up at appropriate local times. This is useful after a westerly journey of up to eight time zones, but is less likely to encourage rapid readjustment after travelling eastwards.

● After flying east any distance, or after flying more than five time zones west, consider taking melatonin supplements (see page 157) at bedtime (new local time) for four nights. This may help reset your body clock, but should be avoided if you are on SSRI anti-depressants, or are pregnant.

● Avoid alcohol when flying east, as alcohol delays the body clock.

● Promote alertness when travelling west with stimulating aromatherapy oils such as citrus, mint and rosemary. Promote sleepiness when travelling east with relaxing oils such as lavender, ylang ylang and sandalwood. Smell the oil in the bottle, or put a few drops in some hand cream.

Migraine

This severe one-sided headache may be associated with nausea and vomiting. There may be a warning 'aura' such as a blind spot; zigzag, flashing light; or an elated feeling. A very few people develop temporary paralysis or loss of speech. The mechanism seems to be a sudden fall in serotonin, dilating blood vessels and encouraging them to leak and become inflamed. Triggers include bright or glaring light, flashing light (perhaps of particular wavelengths), certain visual patterns (such as stripes), stress, noise, certain weather, hunger, a low blood-sugar, and food sensitivity. Some women get it on the Pill, before a period, or with a pregnancy problem called pre-eclampsia.

How light and colour can help

1. For flicker-sensitive migraine, avoid flashing lights such as from the side window of a rapidly moving vehicle, strobing disco lights, a flickering fluorescent tube, or a TV, computer or cinema screen. For problems from a VDU, try Freshlite flicker-screening glasses (see page 156).

2. Individually chosen tinted lenses (such as blue, green, yellow, orange, orange-brown or rose pink) may prevent over-stimulation of certain visual-cortex cells by filtering out particular wavelengths. Choosing the colour is a matter of trial and error. Experiment to see whether putting the glasses on at the beginning of a migraine cures it quickly enough, or whether you need to wear them all the time.

3. If sensitive to bright light, wear sunglasses when entering sunlight.

4. For pre-menstrual migraine, help balance hormone levels by going out in bright light each day for at least 30 minutes in the two weeks before a period.

5. Consider trying a mask that flashes red light for 15 minutes a day. This is most likely to be successful for those who experience an aura; experiment to see if it's more helpful used every day or just when the aura begins.

6. For stress-related migraine, use visual-ization to help you relax.

Other tips

● Press with a fingertip between the eyebrows for 15 seconds.

● Take a cold shower, or put a cold compress or ice pack on your head.

● Eat oily fish three times a week, drink a cup of ginger tea once or twice daily, and identify any suspected food sensitivity.

● Eat feverfew leaves in a sandwich, or take feverfew tablets.

Doctors may also recommend painkillers; preventive therapy with daily aspirin or propanolol; a serotonin-boosting drug such as sumatriptan; or, for menstrual migraine, oestrogen skin patches.

Dyslexia

This is a specific difficulty with reading, spelling and, perhaps, writing or numbers. One possible cause is sensitivity of the brain cells to bright light or particular light wavelengths (colours); flickering bright or coloured light may be worst. Light sensitivity may also cause headaches and dizziness One possible reason is a shortage of certain essential fatty acids in the brain and eyes; another is brain damage.

Confusingly, this sort of light sensitivity is called scotopic sensitivity syndrome, though 'scotopic' strictly refers to night vision (mediated by rods), whereas dyslexic light sensitivity can be to coloured light (mediated by cones), as well as to brightness, black-white contrast, and glare (mediated by rods).

How light and colour can help

1. Try reading through a transparent tinted sheet (overlay). If you have a colour sensitivity, the right tint may help by cutting out irritating wavelengths, so letters or numbers become clearer and stop jiggling, wobbling, pulsating, tilting, stretching, overlapping, 'fizzing', reversing, rotating, or seeming to fall from the page.

2. If an overlay helps, an orthoptist with the right equipment (a colorimeter) can confirm colour sensitivity and prescribe precision-tinted lenses. Some people find blue-green best, others pink, yellow, or green, but a small change can remove any benefit. The Institute of Optometry offers information, testing and coloured overlays, and the Irlen Centre, colour-sensitivity tests (see page 156.
3. See whether dyslexia improves in non-fluorescent lighting.
4. Some children improve with eye exercises (details from an orthoptist).
5. The British Dyslexia Association (see page 156) has a leaflet, 'Eyes and dyslexia' .

Other tips

● Eat more foods rich in zinc, and a good balance of omega-3 and omega-6 fatty acids.
● Consider a daily supplement of essential fatty acids.

Teachers or doctors may also recommend special education programmes geared to the individual's needs.

Attention deficit disorder (ADD)

Some children can't keep still and concentrate. This makes learning difficult and can disrupt relationships. The cause is unclear, but one possible trigger is electric light that contains too much or too little of certain light wavelengths. Other possibilities include stress, hearing or eyesight defects, an overactive thyroid, certain foods and food additives, and brain damage.

How light and colour can help

1. If holidays make your child better, the colour balance or flicker of the classroom's fluorescent tube could be to blame. Discuss installing full-spectrum lighting.

2. Preliminary research suggests flashing light therapy may help.

Other tips

● Provide a healthy diet, with plenty of foods rich in omega-3 and omega-6 fatty acids, and consider giving these as a supplement.

● Keep a food diary for a month to see whether any foods increase hyperactivity. If so, eliminate them one at a time for two or three weeks each. If a food is a major part of the child's diet, do this with a doctor's or dietitian's guidance.

● Do a four-week trial of a diet free from colourings and other additives.

● If stress is a factor, get help with effective management from a doctor, counsellor or parent-support group.

● Brush up on parenting skills with a book or course.

Doctors may also recommend methylphenidate hydrochloride (Ritalin); however, there is no good evidence that it is effective, and it causes side effects in up to one in two children.

Parkinson's disease

This means brain cells that produce the neurotransmitter dopamine have degenerated and become underactive. Other cells try to compensate by becoming overactive. The result may be shaking hands, stiff and slow movements, constipation, poor balance, forgetfulness, confusion, depression, intellectual decline and personality change.

Triggers of Parkinson's – or 'parkinsonism', which has similar symptoms as a result of dopamine receptors being blocked – include arterial disease, carbon monoxide or pesticide poisoning, certain drugs (such as metoclopramide for nausea, and chlorpromazine for schizophrenia) and genetic mutation.

How light and colour can help

1. Green-tinted lenses were once reported to ease symptoms, though this has not been followed up. They block red and yellow light, so perhaps certain brain cells could be oversensitive to these wavelengths. There is no good evidence that they help, but it would be easy to try for a few weeks.

2. Sleep problems may result from a disturbed body clock, and may respond to more daylight, brighter electric light, and morning use of a light visor or box.

Other tips

● Eat plenty of foods rich in antioxidant beta-carotene and vitamins C and E.

● Try boosting dopamine with supplements of tyrosine (an amino acid in animal protein, beans, nuts, and seeds) and NADH (niacinamide adenine dinucleotide hydrogen, a form of vitamin B3, from FSC Vitamins (see page 157).

● Take recommended precautions with pesticides.

● Take regular exercise and don't smoke, to help prevent arterial disease.

● Have gas applicances serviced annually to prevent carbon monoxide leaking.

● Avoid St John's wort, which can interfere with dopamine balance.

Doctors may also recommend L-dopa or more modern drugs, or surgery to destroy overactive areas. Researchers are trying brain 'pacemakers' to stimulate underactive areas, implants of stem cells or genetically engineered nerve cells, nerve-cell growth-factor injections, dopamine-gene therapy; nicotine-type drugs that won't encourage arterial disease (as smoking does), and drugs resembling ecstasy, which causes a massive serotonin release.

Seizures

Also known as fits or convulsions, these result from bursts of chaotic electrical activity from part of the brain. Many people know one is coming because of a warning feeling, such as restlessness or irritability. Some dogs know instinctively when their owner is about to have one. The cause is an over-sensitivity of the brain. Early-life triggers include brain damage from an accident, abnormality, or lack of oxygen before, during or after birth. Other triggers include flickering and patterned light, loud noise, anxiety, anger, fatigue, certain foods (such as wheat), a nutrient deficiency, alcohol, changing hormone levels, certain drugs, certain pesticides, and exposure to particular electromagnetic frequencies.

How light and colour can help
If you have flicker-sensitive seizures:
1. Avoid exposure to flashing light. This could be from, for example, a faulty and flickering fluorescent tube, a TV or VDU screen, strobe lighting in a disco, a very old movie, looking at an escalator, or through the side window of a rapidly moving vehicle, or at sunlight through a canopy of leaves. You may find you can watch TV safely if you cover one eye, or get a high-frequency (100 hertz) TV or one with a smaller screen.
2. Glasses with lenses of a particular tint (such as rose or orange-yellow) might help by cutting out irritating wavelengths. For problems from a VDU, try Freshlite flicker-screening glasses (see page 156).

Other tips
● Eat foods rich in vitamins B6 and E, copper, magnesium and selenium.
● For stress-induced seizures, learn to manage stress more effectively. Also, choose an essential oil that you find relaxing or, for fatigue-induced seizures, choose one you find stimulating. Ask someone to massage you regularly with this oil (six drops in a tablespoon of sweet almond oil). As you relax or become more alert during these massages, you'll come to associate these feelings with the oil's scent. Always keep a small bottle with you and smell the oil if you think you're about to have a seizure.

Doctors may also recommend anti-epilepsy medication. Since certain medications make the Pill less reliable, you may need to discuss contraception. One new treatment involves vagal nerve stimulation: an electronic gadget implanted in the chest prevents some people's seizures by stimulating the vagus in the neck every 5–15 minutes.

Multiple sclerosis (MS)

Possible symptoms of this nerve disorder include pins and needles, weakness, fatigue, trouble trying to talk, eye pain, blurred sight, incontinence and, at worst, paralysis. MS results from patches of inflammation and destruction ('demyelination') of a fatty substance, myelin, which covers many nerves; the nerves may also be damaged and scarred. Myelin normally insulates nerves so that the electric currents that carry messages can't leak. Damage to nerves makes them unreliable at making muscles work and providing information about touch, temperature and other sensations.

Twice as many women as men have MS. Of every 10 people affected, one has occasional mild attacks but is otherwise well, or almost well; four in 10 remain slightly disabled between attacks, while the others become progressively more disabled.

The usual cause of MS is autoimmune attack, when antibodies mistakenly turn against myelin, believing it to be foreign. Suspected triggers include early childhood viral infections, and trauma. Bright daylight seems to reduce the risk because the nearer to the equator you live, the lower is your risk. People in Britain are 100 times more likely to have MS than those who live near the equator, and people living in Scotland have five times the risk of those in England and Wales. One unproven explanation is that the increased amounts of vitamin D produced in the skin by the action of UV in sunlight may help prevent MS. However, adults who have moved from one country to another still have the same risk of MS they had in the first country, whereas children who move acquire the risk of those in their new country. So if sunlight is important for preventing MS, it may be that you need it when you are young.

How light and colour can help

It won't do any harm, and might help, to spend more time outside in bright daylight.

Other tips

● Eat a healthy diet with a good balance of omega-3 and omega-6 fatty acids.
● Consider taking a multi-mineral and vitamin supplement, and a supplement of omega-3 and omega-6 fatty acids.
● Identify any suspected food sensitivity, and avoid any culprit foods.
● Learn how to use more effective stress management.
● Unproven therapies which may be worth discussing with your doctor include high-pressure oxygen, the removal of dental amalgam fillings and, for women, hormone replacement therapy (HRT).
● Some people with MS find cannabis reduces muscle pains. However, there have been only three small uncontrolled trials of tetrahydrocannabinol, the substance which creates the 'high', and we need better evidence to be sure.

Doctors may also recommend steroids, gammaglobulin or a newish and expensive drug, beta interferon.

Immunity and general wellbeing

Obesity

Losing weight isn't usually too much of a problem but nine in 10 slimmers regain their old weight within a year and some become heavier. The main goal is to stay slim.

How light and colour can help

Winter depression (seasonal affective disorder or SAD)

This can make you crave sweet, starchy foods (especially in the late afternoon and evening), or comfort-eat because you feel low.

1. Get more bright outdoor daylight, preferably sunlight, to help balance serotonin and other neurotransmitters and hormones.
2. Brighten electric lighting.
3. Consider using a light visor or box.
4. Consider regular sunbed sessions.

Comfort eating

1. Go out in bright light each day to boost your levels of 'feel-good' substances called endorphins, and help balance neurotrans-mitters such as serotonin.
2. See whether choosing clothes or flowers of a particular colour makes you feel better. Identify how this colour makes you feel, as this may be what you crave when you comfort eat. If so, identifying your need may help you to meet it in a non-destructive way.
3. Consider wearing a flashing-light device – a mask programmed to flash red light – for up to 30 minutes a day to aid relaxation. In one study many women who used such a mask unexpectedly lost weight.
4. Consider using Aura-Soma colour therapy.
5. Use visualization to aid relaxation.

Any obesity

1. Get more bright outdoor daylight or, preferably, sunlight, as UV stimulates the thyroid, which helps burn calories.
2. Consider having regular sunbeds.

Other tips

● Take 30 minutes' daily exercise, which burns calories at the time, raises your metabolic rate for hours and helps prevent comfort eating.

● Eat regularly so that you don't get so hungry you stuff yourself with easy-to-prepare sweet, fatty or starchy food. And permanently change the way you eat so that you don't diet repeatedly. Eat more low-calorie, high-fibre food, such as vegetables and fruit, and less high-calorie food. Avoid sugary, starchy, fatty 'junk food', as it contains few other nutrients. Because you have a lot of fat in your body, you need plenty of foods rich in antioxidants (such as beta-carotene, vitamins C and E, selenium, zinc and plant pigments) to prevent free radicals damaging the fats and encouraging arterial disease and cancer. Finally, aim for an average loss of just under 0.5–1kg (1–2lb) a week.

● Consider taking an evening supplement of melatonin, or of 5HT (5-hydroxytryptophan, used to make serotonin which, in turn, makes melatonin – (but not if you are on SSRI antidepressants or are pregnant.

● Drink plenty, because even slight dehydration reduces the metabolic rate.

● Learn to manage stress effectively; if comfort-eating is a problem, list things to do instead of reaching for food whenyou are finding that times are tough.

Doctors may also recommend

Orlistat, a drug which reduces fat absorption, or sibutramine, a new drug that helps the body burn more calories.

Bulimia

This is the habit of bingeing, and vomiting or taking laxatives. The trigger is generally stress. You want to improve matters and cope with sadness, loneliness, anger or fear, yet feel powerless. So you eat compulsively or go on a diet, either of which causes a craving for sweet, starchy, fatty food. You then binge and feel out of control again. Afterwards you reassert control (and, perhaps, punish yourself) by vomiting or taking laxatives. All this disrupts body chemistry, which makes it difficult to recognize hunger and fullness, and encourages further binges.

Bulimia involves craving carbohydrates and fats – foods also craved by people with winter depression (SAD), in whom a lack of light disrupts neurotransmitters. Many people with bulimia have symptoms like those of SAD. The disrupted body chemistry associated with bulimia probably improves with bright light too, because light therapy halved the number of bouts of bulimia in one study. Some people with bulimia also have tummy ache, tooth decay from erosion of enamel by stomach acid when vomiting, frequent throat infections, absent periods, bloating and fatigue.

How light and colour can help

1. Go outside in bright light each day for as long as you can.

2. Have bright lighting indoors.

3. Consider using a light visor or box each day.

4. Pay special attention to the colour of your clothes, or the flowers you choose; this might help you recognize underlying emotions and express them in non-destructive ways, or simply help by giving pleasure. Aura-Soma may help, too.

5. Use visualization to imagine yourself feeling better.

Other tips

● Take daily aerobic exercise to make you feel better.

● Eat healthy, appetizing meals rich in low-glycaemic-index foods, calcium, magnesium, zinc, vitamins B and C, and a good balance of omega-3s and omega-6s.

● Learn to manage stress more effectively and in a non-damaging way.

Doctors may also recommend cognitive-behavioural psychotherapy to help you understand your circumstances differently and change your behaviour. The addition of antidepressants (such as SSRIs – selective serotonin reuptake inhibitors, which increase serotonin's availablility) is sometimes even more helpful.

Cancer

Cancer cells form repeatedly throughout life and while most are quickly destroyed by the immune system, others multiply uncontrollably and may destroy adjacent tissues, grow into a tumour, spread and kill. Each cancer has its own risk factors, but increasing age applies to most. Cancer is often encouraged by factors that lower immunity, such as an unhealthy diet, smoking, stress, too little exercise, and too much or too little light. For example:

● Skin cancer can result from over-exposure to UV.

● Non-Hodgkin's lymphoma is more likely the nearer the equator you live; it is more likely in those who have skin cancer.

● There is some evidence that UV may directly help protect against breast cancer by encouraging cancer cells to 'commit suicide' (a process called apoptosis).

● People living furthest away from the equator have at least two and a half times the risk of breast, colon, prostate and ovary cancer compared with those near the equator. This could be due to a lack of vitamin D from too little UV on the skin – researchers say that vitamin D helps regulate the rate at which cells divide, so it might limit cancer-cell multiplication; certainly women with breast cancer are more likely to have a low vitamin-D level. Or it could be associated with a lack of melatonin from the pineal glands.

● The breast-cancer risk is raised in long-haul aircrew and frequent flyers. This may be due to frequent jet-lag disturbing their sleep-wake cycle, so lowering their melatonin production.

Exposure to ionizing radiation at high altitudes may also be a cancer risk.

● Breast cancer is more commonly diagnosed in winter.

How light and colour can help

1. Sunbathe in bright daylight, preferably sunlight. As long as you don't burn, this may boost your immunity by lifting your spirits, and by UV triggering vitamin D production. If you have skin cancer, avoid bright daylight on your skin.

2. Consider using bright light from a light visor or box to lift spirits and boost immunity; if you have skin cancer, check it doesn't give off UV.

3. Boost melatonin, a potent antioxidant, with a good sleep-wake cycle, sleeping in the dark at night and staying awake in the light by day. This may be especially useful for breast cancer and malignant melanoma.

4. Surgeons sometimes remove cancers with laser light.

5. Photodynamic therapy is proving useful for some cancers of the head, neck, mouth, oesophagus, larynx, stomach, lung, colon, pancreas, bladder, vulva, prostate, ovary and skin. It's usually done with a low-power red laser light, but isn't yet generally available.

6. Visualize white cells destroying your cancer cells.

Other tips

These natural therapies sometimes slow the progression of cancers that haven't spread, and very occasionally reverse or cure them. In people with advanced cancer they may prolong life and improve its quality.

● Eat more foods rich in plant hormones, which can occupy oestrogen receptors on cells and discourage oestrogen-sensitive cancers such as many breast cancers.

● Eat more foods rich in calcium, to discourage breast cancer, and fibre, to lower raised oestrogen.

● Eat a good balance of omega-3 and omega-6 fatty acids; this encourages a healthy balance of the nerve-message chemical, serotonin, as well as of prostaglandins and other substances which boost immunity; and reduces the chronic inflammation associated with some cancers.

● Eat more foods rich in salicylates to inhibit the production of certain prostaglandins which can stimulate cancer growth and suppress immunity.

● Eat more foods rich in antioxidants such as beta-carotene, vitamins C and E, selenium and flavonoids; these fight free radicals (hyperactive oxygen particles) which encourage new cancers to begin.

● Eat three helpings a week of oily fish; one of its omega-3 fatty acids, eicosapentanoic acid, can reverse the weight loss that occurs in one in four people dying from cancer.

● Have five to nine daily helpings of fruit and vegetables for their various cancer-fighting substances. For example, tomatoes cooked in fat have high amounts of a potent flavonoid called lycopene. Garlic contains a natural breast-cancer inhibitor called S-allomercapto-cysteine, and onions contain similar substances. Cruciferous vegetables (cabbage, broccoli, Brussels sprouts) contain glucosinolates, which help kill cancer cells. Citrus peel oil contains various anti-cancer substances: liquidize a whole citrus fruit, and either drink it or incorporate it into a fruit pudding or other recipe. Grape skins contain resveratrol, which can inhibit all stages of cancer growth. Cherries contain ellagic acid which blocks an enzyme needed for cancer cell growth. And ginger and turmeric supply helpful antioxidants.

● Each day drink several cups of green tea, because its polyphenols encourage cells with damaged DNA to die.

● Identify any suspected food sensitivity. Researchers are beginning to suspect that some cancers may improve when no longer exposed to substances called lectins in certain foods to which a person is sensitive.

● Try visualization, a mind game in which you imagine your immune cells successfully destroying the cancer.

● Boost your immunity by finding things to laugh at and enjoy, and using effective stress-management strategies.

Doctors may also recommend anti-cancer drugs (chemotherapy), surgery and radiotherapy.

Lupus

Systemic lupus erythematosus, to give it its full name, is an autoimmune ('self-allergic') condition. Normally, our antibodies protect us from foreign proteins in bacteria, pollens, foods, cancer cells, etc. Sometimes, though, some sort of trigger – such as stress or too much sun – causes gene mutation in certain

antibodies embedded in immune cells. Normally, such immune cells self-destruct. But if the immune system isn't working properly, this doesn't happen. Abnormal antibodies may then 'change sides' and attack normal tissue. Other autoimmune diseases include rheumatoid arthritis, insulin-dependent diabetes, Hashimoto's thyroiditis, systemic sclerosis (thickening and tightening of connective tissue), glomerulonephritis (a type of kidney inflammation), AIDS and, perhaps, endometriosis and premature ovarian failure.

With lupus, abnormal antibodies make blood vessels inflamed. This 'vasculitis' can affect many parts, causing fatigue, fever, weight-loss, joint pain, and a light-sensitive rash on the nose and cheeks. Other possibilities include mouth ulcers, pleurisy, poor circulation, kidney damage, aching muscles, hair loss and anaemia. There is also a raised risk of diabetes, an underactive thyroid, seizures, a dry mouth and depression.

Lupus is more common in women, especially after an early menopause. Possible triggers include stress, a poor diet, lack of exercise, too much sunshine, hormonal change, infection, certain drugs and (though unproven) sensitivity to substances called lectins found in such foods as wheat, potatoes, tomatoes, peanuts and alfalfa sprouts.

Lupus tends to come and go, and may run in families. One type encourages migraine, frequent miscarriage (due to blood-clots in the placenta), heart attack, strokes and other brain damage.

How light and colour can help

1. If you have a rash, avoid sunlight or use sunblock.
2. Eat more foods rich in plant pigments, including beta-carotene.

Other tips

● Aim to identify and avoid triggers.
● Eat a healthy, varied diet, with plenty of foods rich in folic acid, vitamins C and E, copper (liver, nuts, seeds, beans, fish, wholegrains), magnesium, selenium, zinc and omega-3 fatty acids.
● Identify any suspected food sensitivity.
● Consider taking glucosamine sulphate – some experts suspect that this amino-sugar may prevent damage by lectins.
● Exercise daily, pacing yourself carefully.
● Learn to manage stress more effectively, if necessary.
● Consider boosting immunity with a three-month course of echinacea and astragalus.

Doctors may also recommend anti-nuclear antibody blood tests. *For mild lupus* – painkillers and non-steroidal anti-inflammatory drugs. *For a severe condition* – steroids and immunity suppressing, cytotoxic (cell killing) and anti-malarial drugs. One experimental treatment is stem-cell transplantation, which involves removing bone marrow cells, treating the person with immunity-suppressing drugs, then replacing the cells.

Sleep problems

Difficulty getting to sleep can result from anxiety, depression, excitement, indigestion, pain, discomfort, certain foods or drinks, heat, cold, noise and light. Waking soon after is often due to anxiety or noise. Disturbed sleep may result from noise, nightmares or menopausal hot flushes. Waking unrefreshed usually reflects insufficient time dreaming or sleeping deeply. Early waking can result from dawn light or depression. Many sleep problems are associated with an imbalance of neurotransmitters such as serotonin, noradrenaline and adrenaline, which can all be influenced by light.

How light and colour can help

1. Decorate the bedroom a colour you find relaxing.
2. Keep light levels low for several hours before bedtime.
3. Line curtains to reduce dawn light.
4. If you sleep badly on shift work, see pages 141–2.
5. If you have jet-lag, see pages 142–3.
6. If a person has Alzheimer's, see pages 140–1.
7. Help recognize and express any difficult emotions by thinking what the colours you choose for clothes or flowers symbolize.
8. Visualize relaxing scenes.
9. Researchers are investigating whether a flashing-light mask helps. If you try, begin with 13 flashes a second, then turn it down as you become sleepy.

Other tips

● Take 30 minutes' exercise around five or six hours before bedtime.
● Eat more foods rich in calcium, magnesium, manganese, zinc and vitamin B. Lettuce, rosemary and thyme may help too.
● Have your last meal early and keep later snacks small, light, carbohydrate-rich and cheese-free.
● Consider taking supplements of zinc in the morning, and, in the evening, calcium, magnesium and either melatonin or 5-HTP (5-hydroxytryptophan – used to make serotonin which, in turn, is used to make melatonin). Avoid melatonin and 5-HTP if you are taking SSRI (selective serotonin reuptake inhibitor) antidepressants or St John's wort, or if you are pregnant or breastfeeding.
● Don't over-indulge in alcohol in the evening if this interferes with sleep.
● Avoid cocoa, cola and coffee and tea (unless decaffeinated) after 4pm; drink chamomile, lemon balm, linden (lime) blossom, vervain or hop tea instead.
● Consider taking the herbal remedies valerian and passiflora an hour before bedtime.
● Don't sleep in the evening.
● Don't smoke in the evening, as this may reduce melatonin.
● Have a warm, lavender-oil scented bath before retiring.
● Learn effective stress-management strategies if necessary.
● Check your bed, bed covers and bedroom are comfortable.
● Use earplugs if noise interferes with sleep.

Doctors may also recommend drugs to relax you or aid sleep.

Diabetes

Someone with untreated diabetes has a high blood-sugar level because they either produce little or no insulin, or don't respond normally to insulin ('insulin resistance').

Type 1 usually starts suddenly, from the age of 10–16, with thirst, frequent urination and weight loss. Untreated, it kills. Type 2 usually comes on slowly in later life, with unexplained thirst or fatigue, blurred vision and frequent passing of dilute urine. This is becoming increasingly common in children and adults as they get fatter. Sometimes it's provoked by infection, by steroid teatment or by pregnancy. Untreated, or poorly treated, it damages arteries, possibly leading to cataracts, damaged retinas, kidneys and nerves (causing pins and needles and numbness), leg ulcers and heart attacks or strokes.

How light and colour can help

1. Get more sunlight. This lowers the melatonin level, and hence reduces the blood sugar. Also, vitamin D made in the skin by UV helps cells respond better to insulin.
2. Consider replacing electric lights, especially 'warm' ones, with full-spectrum fluorescent lights without UV-blocking diffusers, as red wavelengths can raise the blood sugar, whereas UV lowers it. This sort of fluorescent light gives around 10 per cent of UV and 90 per cent of visible light, the same proportion as in sunlight.

3. In bad weather, consider having UV sunbed treatments (though not if you have risk factors for skin cancer, see page 92).
4. A new device that measures blood-sugar – the Glucowatch Biographer, see www.glucowatch.com – means that people who use insulin no longer have to prick their finger several times a day to get a drop of blood to check their blood sugar. The device uses a beam of infrared light on the skin to assess the blood-sugar level.

Other tips

● Check your sugar level with regular urine or blood tests.
● Take a daily half-hour's brisk exercise to halve your risk of diabetes.
● Stop smoking, to help protect your arteries.
● Lose excess weight and keep it off.
● Eat a healthy diet with at least five daily helpings of fruit and vegetables (including onions, garlic, beans and lentils). Include wholegrains (especially oats) and foods rich in vitamins B, C and E, chromium (go for beans, mushrooms and brown basmati rice) and zinc. Eat a good balance of essential fats.
● Be aware of whether each food you eat has a high or low glycaemic index (GI, see page 109). High-GI foods make the body's blood-sugar level rise rapidly and to a higher level, while low-GI foods make iit rise more slowly and to a lower level. When you eat anything other than a low-GI food, it's best to eat some low GI-food (such as any protein, green vegetables and certain fruits) at the same time, as this 'dilutes' the blood-sugar-raising effect. Eat high-GI

foods (such as bread and cereals) only in small amounts.

● Consider taking supplements of vitamin B complex (to help sugar metabolism), vitamins C and E, proanthocyanidins and quercetin (antioxidants to protect the eyes), and chromium picolinate (to help stabilize blood sugar in type-2 diabetes).

● A daily 25g (⅘oz) of powdered fenugreek seeds may help prevent arterial disease.

Doctors may also recommend anti-diabetic drugs or insulin for type-2 diabetes, and insulin injections for type 1. If you have type 1 you have a raised risk of being sensitive to gluten and developing coeliac disease; one study estimated the risk at one in 20. So some experts recommend routine blood tests for anti-endomysial antibodies; if positive, a bowel biopsy can confirm the diagnosis. In coeliac disease, a protein called gluten (in wheat, barley, rye and, perhaps, oats) damages the bowel lining and can cause poor digestion, anaemia, weight loss, infertility, osteoporosis, diabetes and a raised risk of bowel cancer; the treatment is to avoid gluten.

If your risk of type 2 is high, you'll need an annual blood-sugar check, because it often doesn't trigger obvious problems for a long time, yet can cause unnoticed damage. One risk factor is being overweight: three out of four sufferers are very overweight and have the most dangerous distribution of body fat – around their middle. Other risks include heavy smoking, high blood pressure, Asian or Afro-Caribbean ancestry, pregnancy diabetes, and diabetes in the family.

Convalescence

Whatever's been wrong, these simple tips will speed your recovery or, at least, help you feel better.

How light and colour can help

1. Exposure to bright daylight promotes recovery. The pleasure of sunbathing boosts 'feel-good' endorphins, and relaxing in the sun lowers stress hormones; both these boost immunity. Sunlight on the skin and in the eyes can also help by rebalancing any hormones and neurotransmitters disrupted by illness.
2. Bright light early in the morning can help reset a body clock disrupted by being inside a long time.
3. Visualizing yourself being better may help you get better, perhaps because it gives you hope and a goal, or because the relief which comes with thinking about your recovery boosts endorphins.

Other tips

● Think what other forms of 'tlc' – (tender loving care – might aid recovery.

Helplist

Aura-soma
www.aura-soma.com

Bates Association £1 for information to
PO Box 25, Shoreham-by-Sea, West Sussex BN43 6ZF (01273 422090)

Behavioural optometry preventive care for visual problems, consideration of visual aspects of learning problems, vision improvement techniques and emotional aspects of poor vision. Only a few practitioners.
UK - Shaylers Vision Centre, 25 West Street, Wareham, Dorset BH20 4JS (01929 553928)
www.visiontherapy.co.uk
USA – College of Optometrists in Vision Development, 888 268 3770; www.covd.org

Bioforce UK, Irvine, Ayrshire, Scotland (01294 277344) can supply Seven Herb Cream for eczema.

Bioptron polarized-light therapy device
Glowing Health Ltd, Jaysforde House, College Road, Newton Abbot, Devon TQ12 1EF (01626 336 337)
USA – Zepter International USA Inc, 8400 River Road, North Bergen NJ 07047 (201 453 0637)
www.bioptron.com

British Dyslexia Association Eyes and Dyslexia leaflet 0118 966 8271

British Orthokeratology Society large sae for information to
7 Devonshire Street, London W1N 1FT

Cerium Visual Technologies Ltd list of optometrists with equipment for selecting tinted lenses
Cerium Technology Park, Appledore Road, Tenterden, Kent TN30 7DE (01580 765211)

CoCrysto torch for very localized colour therapy
Theo Gimbel, Hygeia College of Colour Therapy, Brook House, Avening, Tetbury, Gloucestershire GL8 8NS (0145 383 2150)

Colour Me Beautiful image consultancy
66 Abbey Business Centre, Ingate Place, London SW8 3NS (0207 627 5211)

Coloured and UV-blocking sleeves for fluorescent tubes from
Cocoon Light, Formatt Filters Ltd, Unit 23, Aberaman Park Industrial Estate, Aberdare, Mid Glamorgan, CF44 6DA, Wales (01685 870979), and Transformation Tubes, 118 Winkworth Road, Banstead, Surrey SM7 2QR (01737 373483)

Colourwash Lighting System floor, wall or ceiling fitments producing dimmable and mixable colours from Isometrix Lighting and Design, 8 Glass House Yard, London EC1A 4JN (020 7253 2888)
- For Metamorfosi fitments providing various combinations of colours
Artemide, 106 Great Russell Street, London WC1B 3NB (020 7631 5200)
- For Translulu fluorescent tube plus diffuser surrounded by a controllable coloured roll
Tasque, 63 Dundale Road, Tring, Herts HP23 5BX (01442 822601)

Dermalux light box producing red and blue light for acne
99 Windmill Street, Gravesend, Kent DA12 1LE (0800 0722122)

Eye Care Information Service information about eye care and 'eyewear'
PO Box 131, Market Rasen, Lincolnshire, LN8 5TS (01673 857847)
www.eyecare-information-service.org.uk

Freshlite glasses anti-flicker lenses for flicker-sensitive headaches,

eyestrain, migraine and epilepsy
www.freshlite.com

Full-spectrum lights
Full Spectrum Lighting Ltd., Unit 48, Marlow Road, Stokenchurch, High Wycombe, Buckinghamshire HP14 3QT (01494 448727)
- For flicker-free fluorescent LifeEnergy Biolights that fit incandescent light fittings
Higher Nature, Burwash Common, East Sussex TN19 7BR (01435 882880)
- USA for Ott Light
Ott Light Systems, Inc., 306 East Coat Street, Santa Barbara, CA 93101 (800 234 3725)
- USA for Vita-Lite
Duro-Test Corporation, 9 Law Drive, Fairfield, NJ 07007 (800 289 3876)

Hygeia College of Colour Therapy CoCrysto torch, Eye Healing lamp (coloured light for treating cataracts, glaucoma, etc.), training, treatment See under CoCrysto torch, above.

Institute of Optometry information, testing, and coloured overlays for people with dyslexia
56-62 Newington Causeway, London SE1 6DS (0171 407 4183)

Interior design online from
Interior Studio Ltd, Unit 11, Manvers Business Park, High Hazles Road, Cotgrave, Nottingham NG12 3GZ (0115 989 9947)
www.interiorstudio.com

Irlen Centre colour-sensitivity testing and a book, *Reading by the Colors* (also available through www.amazon.co.uk)
137 Bishop's Mansions, Stevenage Road, London SW6 6DX (0171 736 5752)

Jacob Liberman author of Light, *Medicine of the Future* (Bear & Co, $16.95), now interested in light as a metaphor for spiritual enlightenment
www.jacobliberman.com

Light boxes produce bright light of up to 10,000 lux
Outside In (Cambridge) Ltd., 21 Scotland Road Estate, Dry Drayton, Cambridge CB3 8AT (01954 211 955)
www.outsidein.co.uk
- SAD Lightbox Co Ltd, Unit 48, Marlow Road, Stokenchurch, High Wycombe, Buckinghamshire HP14 3QT (01494 448727)
www.sad.uk.com
- USA – Bio-Brite, Inc, 4350 East West Highway, Suite 401W, Bethesda, MD 20814; toll-free 800 621 5483; 301 961-5940
www.members.aol.com/biobrite/bbhome.htm

Light masks for flashing red light in eyes
LightMask, 0870 516 8143
www.lightmask.com or www.light-therapy.com
- US - RelaxEase (also sold elsewhere as Relaxmate)
Tools for Exploration, 9755 Independence Avenue, Chatsworth, CA 91311 4318 (888 748 6657)
International: (+1) 818 885-9090)
www.toolsforexploration.com

Light visors produce bright light up to 3000 lux.
Outside In, see under Light boxes, above.
- US – BioBrite, Inc, see under Light boxes, above.

Melatonin buy synthetic melatonin, not 'natural' melatonin from cows' pineal glands, because of concern about BSE infection. Unsuitable if pregnant or breast-feeding, or on medication other than minor painkillers and the Pill. This cannot be sold legally in the UK, as proof of its safety is lacking, but it is available from PharmWest Ireland (freephone 00 800 8923 8923) and from PharmWest US, 520 Washington Boulevard, no. 401, Marina del Ray CA 90292 (310 301 4015) Also available over the counter in the USA and Singapore.

Melissa ointment for cold sores, £5 for 5gr (0.1oz): PO or cheque to Herpes Viruses Association, 41 North Road, London N7 9DP

NADH, a form of vitamin B3 sometimes taken for Parkinson's disease, from FSC Vitamins, Nutrina Ltd, Whitehorse Business Park, Trowbridge, Wiltshire BA14 0XQ (01483 410611)

Natural Vision Instructors
www.visioneducators.org

Nono torch red 660nm pen-torch light. From Innovations catalogue on (0870 908 7070)

Open Your Eyes to Working With VDUs leaflet from
Optical Information Council, 57a Old Woking Road, West Byfleet, Surrey KT14 6LF (Quitline 0800 002200)

Royal National Institute for the Blind
224 Great Portland Street, London W1W 5AA (Helpline 0845 766 9999)
www.rnib.org.uk and www.rnib.org-uk/technology

ScalpBloc sunscreen for bald heads from
Pharmavita, PO Box 3379, London SW18 4WZ (0208 875 2861)

Society for Light Treatment and Biological Rhythms
- USA - PO Box 591687, 174 Cook Street, San Francisco, CA 94159 1687
www.sltbr.org

Syntonic Optometry coloured light therapy through the eyes (optometric phototherapy) for visual problems, including some learning difficulties and squints. Only a few UK practitioners. See Shaylers Vision Centre under Behavioural Optometry.
- US - College of Syntonic Optometry, (717 387 0900); practitioners list from www.syntonicphototherapy.com

Tecno AO magnetic alpha oscillator antenna said to restore alpha brainwave rhythm in people sensitive to a VDU's emf
Tecno AO (UK) Ltd, Draycot Foliat, Swindon, Wiltshire SN4 0HX (01793 741080), www.tecnoaouk.com

To see reading matter magnified on TV Horizon TV Reader ('video mouse' held over printed matter). One of two closed-circuit reading aids offering hands-free variable magnification – Horizon Duo Merit (black and white) and Horizon Duo Multicolour (colour)
Horizon CCTV, 11-12 Lowman Units, Tiverton Business Park, Tiverton, Devon EX16 6SR (01884 254172).
- For a 'video mouse' giving 28x magnification on a big TV
Low Vision Supplies, 2 Finchale Avenue, Billingham, Stockton, Cleveland TS23 2DG (01642 530801)
- Easier-to-read websites for people with poor vision; SETI (search engine technology interface) computer programme
www.SETI-search.com

Trayner glasses
Trayner Pinhole Glasses, 1-2 Athena Avenue, Elgin Drive Industrial Estate, Swindon SN2 6EJ (0800 071 2020)

Tryptophan
PharmWest, see details under Melatonin, above. Available over the counter in the USA and some other countries.

Tubular skylights architectural 'daylight tubes' that bring natural daylight into dark places
www.solaglobal.com and www.natralux.co.uk

Wartner aerosol produces a spray that deep-freezes warts; from Boots, Superdrug and some other pharmacies in the UK.

Index

Photographic acknowledgements

Science Photo Library: pages 2/3, 6/7 & 101 (Cordelia Molloy), 10/11 (Steve Horrell),12/13 (Ralph Eagle), 18/19 (Brian Brake), 20/21 (Adam Hart-Davis), 24/25 (B & C Alexander), 32/33 (NASA), 35 (Simon Fraser), 42/43 (Adam Hart-Davis), 62/63 (M. Lustbader), 70/71 (Luke Dodd), 75 (NASA), 80/81 (Bernhard Edmater)
Arcaid: page 36 (Richard Bryant), 37 (Richard Waite)
Oxford Scientific Films: 26/27 (Richard Packwood), 30/31 (Ian Adams/Garden Image), 38/39 (Lightworker/Garden Image)
Interior Studio Ltd, www.interiorstudio.com 44/45
Guerlain Paris 49 (the Météorites range)
Travel Ink: 51 (Emmanuel Agbaraojo)

Digital Vision 52/53
Getty Images Telegraph: 57 (Jean-Noel Reichel), 59 (Stephanie Rausser), 65 (K. Reid), 66/67 (Kamil Vojnar), 85 (Jamie Baker)
Getty Images Stone: 60/61 (Owen Franken), 77 (Ed Pritchard)
Garden Picture Library: 69 (Jeremy Cockayne), 83 (David Cavagnaro)
London Underground: 78/79
Bioptron: 93
Trayner Pinhole Glasses: 95
Charles Walker Photographic: 99
Flowers and Foliage: 100
Rio Lightmask: 105